Coming of Age
The Education and Development of Young Adolescents

by

Kenneth L. Brighton

A Resource for Educators and Parents

National Middle School Association
Westerville, Ohio

Printed in the United States of America.

Betty Edwards, Executive Director—Jeff Ward, Deputy Executive Director—April Tibbles, Director of Publications—Edward Brazee, Editor, Professional Publications—John Lounsbury, Consulting Editor, Professional Publications—Mary Mitchell, Designer, Editorial Assistant—Dawn Williams, Publications Manager—Lindsay Kronmiller, Graphic Designer—Nikia Reveal, Graphic Designer—Marcia Meade-Hurst, Senior Publications Representative—Peggy Rajala, Publications Marketing/Ad Sales Coordinator

Library of Congress Cataloging-in-Publication Data

Brighton, Kenneth L., date
    Coming of age: the education and development of young adolescents: a resource for educators and parents/by Kenneth L. Brighton
        p. cm.
    Includes bibliographical references.
    ISBN: 978-1-56090-211-9
1. Adolescence. 2. Teenagers. 3. Preteens. 4. Middle school students. I. National Middle School Association. II. Title.
HQ796.B6885 2007
305.235'5--dc22

                                                                2007015668

National Middle School Association
4151 Executive Parkway Suite 300
Westerville, Ohio 43081
p: 614-895-4730   f: 614-895-4750
www.nmsa.org

DEDICATION

To the hundreds of young adolescents who passed through my classroom and taught me that there is no more challenging yet rewarding job than to be a middle level teacher. And to my son, Casey, who taught me that it is much easier to teach and write about young adolescents than to effectively parent them. I am so proud of the young man you have become!

K.L.B.

ACKNOWLEDGMENTS

Few worthy tasks are completed in isolation. So it is with this publication. Numerous individuals have encouraged and inspired me to complete this work. My hope is that those who read these pages will glean a nugget or two that will be useful for teachers, parents, and other advocates of young adolescents.

My former students from Owen Valley Middle School in Spencer, Indiana, provided me with nearly two decades of classroom experience from which I drew heavily as resources for this book. My son, Casey, as well as his friends and peers, have given me a close-up and personal view of early adolescence as well as subjects for some of the case studies. I wish to thank the students at Lamoille Union Middle School in Hyde Park, Vermont, and the Alpha Team of the Shelburne Community School in Shelburne, Vermont, for contributing the student quotes used throughout the text, and the teachers from those two fine schools for permitting students to respond to my survey.

Many professional educators have been instrumental in helping me complete this project. I am delighted to have worked with Drs. John Lounsbury and Ed Brazee, editors of professional publications for National Middle School Association. Their editing and suggestions for improving my manuscript were extremely helpful. Having Chris Stevenson write the foreword is an honor for me. I read much of Dr. Stevenson's work when I was a middle level teacher in the Midwest. Never in my wildest dreams did I ever think that I would become a professional colleague and personal friend with such a renowned middle level scholar. As a teacher educator, I found the writings of Professor John Santrock from the University of Texas most helpful. He provided a framework for how I think about adolescents. I also am grateful to the administration at Johnson State College for granting me a sabbatical leave to complete this project, and to my colleagues in the education department for picking up the slack created by my absence.

I am also deeply indebted to my wife, Maryanne, for her unfailing emotional support and technical assistance. A published writer, she has been invaluable as an editor and proofreader, and in assisting me in unraveling numerous computer glitches. As has been the case throughout our marriage, Maryanne's confidence in my abilities has often surpassed my own and I will always be grateful to her for helping me realize my potential.

—Ken Brighton

CONTENTS

FOREWORD

Countless conversations over 40 years with teachers, adult students, and several friends about recollections from their early adolescent years have revealed one clear and certain theme: *everyone remembers.* Everyone!

I have long been convinced of the usefulness of such inquiries as teachers go about learning about the students with whom they are going to be in close association. Thus, such conversations do not come up serendipitously. I ask directly, because I think it is essential that those of us who have authority in the lives of young adolescents be willing to candidly examine our own personal experience and biases if we are to be able to honestly embrace our students with genuine empathy and respect. Such inquiries are as much a part of a teacher's efforts to understand students as a doctor's inquiry to understand a patient's state of health. It makes perfect sense that we should have extensive professional knowledge of our constituents. Like Professor Harold Hill, the salesman character in *The Music Man*, "you've gotta know the territory." In *Coming of Age: The Education and Development of Young Adolescents*, Ken Brighton has done just that. He definitely knows the territory of young adolescents.

Interestingly, I have also found that a huge majority of people I have asked also mention how interesting it is to revisit this part of their growing up years, even when sometimes their recollections appear to disturb them in the telling. The only people I can recall who either avoided the question or claimed vaguely not to have any memories were inasmuch as I could tell fairly traditional educators who perceived schooling pretty much exclusively about getting across the subject matter. It could be that their tradition of preoccupation with covering and testing content had eased them away from recalling or confronting their own histories. This is mere conjecture, of course. I don't suggest that such memories are comprehensive over several years or that details are factually precise. However, I am always impressed by a tone of personal feeling—a palpable intimacy—which we have toward some of the developmental events that imprinted us in such enduring ways. Perhaps it was the awkward realization of a voice change, one's earliest sexual urges, the troubling recognition of a parent's flaw, the hot rush of realization that a confidence shared in trust with a friend had been betrayed. These conversations include references to personal changes from the timing and pace of physical development to preoccupations with peers to reflections about one's potential for becoming a successful adult. However, after a lifetime of inquiry into these few vital years of the human life span, I have come to believe that teachers of young adolescents must know all that is possible for them to know about their constituents in order to connect with them in enduring, meaningful ways. One's professional knowledge base must range from the general developmental paths of emerging adolescence to the idiosyncrasies of the individuals they purport to educate.

It is truly unfortunate when adults in charge of young adolescents simply don't understand or respect the dynamics of their students' personal lives. It is no surprise that the kids so often say a significant adult "just doesn't understand" or "doesn't get it." They can be speaking about any adult in their lives, including parents and often even their teachers. This lack of understanding of general developmental change might derive from a teacher preparation program that simply didn't adequately address the multifarious developmental changes of late childhood and early adolescence. Sadly it all too often reflects adult indifference to the events of growing up. The good news is that gradually our profession is elevating itself in terms of responsibility to teacher preparation by insisting that new middle level teachers understand the paths of human growth and change that are so manifest during the early adolescent years. Whatever the reason may be for ignorance about child development, it is both possible and necessary for us to continually inform ourselves about the vulnerable young learners in our charge.

This volume is a valuable resource toward understanding the various ways in which human beings continue to evolve and develop over the approximate ages of 10 to 15. We are accustomed to seeing physical differences among boys and girls of the same age. Twelve-year-old boys and girls represent quite a range in terms of weight and height, for example. It is not uncommon for adults' expectations of children to be influenced by the mere physical size of children. Teachers have an advantage when it comes to recognizing differing cognitive maturity; they see these differences manifest every day in classrooms. Somewhat more difficult to discern from superficial interactions is the psychosocial maturity of children. However, just as one sees and assumes physical and intellectual differences, so should one recognize that even when differences in temperament and values and morals are not so visible, they are likewise present and in flux as life experience increasingly becomes such an unrelenting tutor. The most crucial realization of all for teachers, however, is the understanding that none of the changes in adolescence occurs in isolation from other changes. *Coming of Age* does this so well with its three interlocking sections: the domains of development, the contexts of such development, and the well-being of young adolescents. What must not be lost, however, is the essential recognition of the dynamic interactive effects of all growth, always aware that some changes are more obvious and visible than others.

Teachers and parents benefit enormously from understanding what is going on with their young charges. When one understands development in general, then the idiosyncrasies of an individual case make more sense. But however complete one's general knowledge may be, the importance of knowing and respecting individuals is not diminished. The enterprise of education during this time of life has always been and will continue to be grounded in interpersonal relationships among students and between students and adults, be they teachers, coaches, parents, or adult friends. Understanding of the general and the particular are essential, but understanding without concomitant commitment is impotent.

Chris Stevenson
Professor Emeritus
University of Vermont
Pinehurst, North Carolina

INTRODUCTION

Every life stage has its challenges, but most adults would agree that early adolescence is perhaps the most difficult one to successfully navigate. My own personal and professional experience has convinced me that many if not most people find the middle school years to be very difficult. When asked, most adults say that given the chance, they would not want to go back in time and relive their early adolescent years. As a middle school teacher for nearly two decades, I frequently had my sanity questioned since I enjoyed the challenge of working with middle level students. Now that I teach prospective middle level teachers and graduate students, I frequently ask them if they ever "played school" as a child. Students often proudly answer "yes." When I press them further and ask if they ever played "middle school," I usually get a less than enthusiastic response accompanied by groans and rolling eyes. Most adults do not count their middle school years as a favorite time of their lives.

Yet no other age is more important than these years when youth come of age. Young adolescents need and deserve parents and teachers who fully understand them and can help them successfully negotiate the challenges that accompany this transition stage. As they strive for the independence and autonomy that comes with maturation, they still need—and secretly desire—the watchful eye and active involvement of caring adults. Parents, obviously, play the prime role; but middle school teachers are usually next in the line of "significant others." Middle school teachers should have a special affinity for young adolescents and be able to serve as a resource for parents who regularly ask, often in frustration, *What is this middle school doing to our son? He used to be a quiet, compliant, polite, and agreeable child. Now he is loud, argumentative, and rude.*

Obviously, it is not a part of any school's mission to turn model children into incorrigible youngsters. Parents need to recognize that the changes they observe—and endure—are normal, natural, and even necessary behaviors of a youngster in transition from childhood to adolescence. The numerous and rapid changes can often be equally perplexing for the young teens themselves. For adults who work closely with young adolescents, it is essential to try to remember what it was like to be a "tween-ager." I have a large photograph of myself, taken when I was a seventh grader; it hangs on the wall in my office to help me remember what it was like to be 13 years old.

This book is designed specifically to help parents, teachers, youth organization leaders and other adults who work with young adolescents better understand the unique nature of this critical life stage as it is played out in our society. The first section explores the intellectual, social, emotional, moral, and physical characteristics of 10- to 15-year-olds. The second section investigates the major contexts in which young adolescents function, their families, and the general culture. The final section highlights health and wellness issues pertinent to young adolescents as well as possible intervention strategies that can help them live healthy lives.

Young adolescents are neither big children nor small adults. Early adolescence is not a "phase" that simply must be endured until it runs its course. It is a pivotal life stage in which personal values, habits, and attitudes are formed and carried into adulthood. By helping individuals be the best they can be during their middle school years, the adults with whom they associate play key roles in helping young adolescents become caring and ethical citizens as well as high-achieving students and productive members of our society. It is to these ends that this book is devoted. —KLB

Section One

DOMAINS OF DEVELOPMENT

Knowing students well is a key to successfully teaching them—just as parents need to understand their offspring fully to effectively guide their development. Yet, the age of early adolescence, roughly the years between 10 and 15, has only recently been recognized as a distinctive stage and been the subject of research. For too long, schools were organized as elementary for children and secondary for adolescents, completely overlooking what we now know is a particularly critical transitional stage between childhood and full adolescence. Far too many schools and the parents they serve still lack a solid understanding of young adolescent growth and development.

The chapters in this section provide the needed sound, basic information on the unique characteristics of this age group in the major areas of development beginning with the critical intellectual development that is so often overlooked. Then the more noticeable social and emotional development areas are examined followed by information on the dramatic physical development. The last chapter studies young adolescents' moral, religious, and character development. While these domains are considered separately, it is essential to remember that during early adolescence these characteristics are interrelated and interactive. ▪

Young adolescents come in various sizes and shapes and are a gregarious lot.

1.
Intellectual Development

Young adolescents dread hearing relatives or other adults comment "My, how you have grown." Such adults hold an image in their minds of the child the person was at their last encounter. The physical transformation that takes place during early adolescence is so dramatic it elicits comments, while the more subtle intellectual maturation that is also taking place is not noted. But certainly the development of the cognitive abilities of young adolescents is every bit as important as their physical maturation. The maturation process of all the domains is rather sporadic, taking place over varied amounts of time.

Cognitive theory and young adolescents—Jean Piaget

While many theories of learning exist, none has been more influential in the field of education than Jean Piaget's theory of cognitive development. Piaget (1896–1980) was a Swiss-born psychologist who used extensive observations of and interviews with children to construct his theory of how people develop intellectually. Piaget theorized that through experience and exposure to phenomena, individuals form concepts and interpret what they encounter in their environment. For example, toddler Jimmy sees a small four-legged animal covered with short hair, that barks. Jimmy begins to form a blueprint in his mind for the concept of "dog." Piaget called such mental models a *schema*. But as Jimmy matures and gains more experience, he must continually adjust and adapt his existing schema. He encounters a much larger animal with four legs, and long hair, which also barks. The child incorporates this creature into the existing schema and concludes the animal is a dog. The child is able to interpret his experience in a way that fits his existing concept. *Assimilation* is the term Piaget used when one is able to fit a new experience into his existing schema. But at some point, individuals need to expand their schema to make what is reality fit one's perception. To extend the example, Jimmy eventually learns that warm-blooded animals covered with hair give birth to live young and are classified as mammals. Then he reads about an aquatic animal that lays eggs, but is also considered a mammal. The duck-billed platypus is so unusual that Jimmy must now expand his existing schema of mammal to make room for the platypus. Piaget coined the term *accommodation* to refer to such modifications in one's schema to interpret unconventional experiences.

As youngsters mature intellectually, Piaget (1954) proposed that they progress through four stages of cognitive development as they attempt to make sense of their surroundings. The four stages have been widely cited and are outlined below as summarized by Santrock (2005):

- **Sensorimotor Stage** (ages birth–2 years). The infant is usually bound by his senses to interpret his surroundings. Most responses are instinctive and reflexive at birth. Toward the end of the stage, infants are beginning to comprehend rudimentary symbolic thought.

- **Preoperational Stage** (ages 2–7 years). The child's cognitive development is dominated by symbolic thought processes. Vocabulary development and word acquisition flourish at this stage. The child also can represent her understandings by acting out scenarios and through simple drawings. Yet children at this stage can not mentally analyze and synthesize events and situations, a cognitive ability Piaget called *operations*.

- **Concrete Operational Stage** (ages 7–11 years). During this stage youngsters can think logically, especially about ideas and events to which they have had direct exposure. Logical thinking is also possible about concepts that are real and relevant to their experience rather than hypothetical. The concrete operational thinker is concerned for the first time with *why* events occur and is now able to perform *operations* that were impossible during earlier stages.

- **Formal Operational Stage** (ages 11–15 years). Young adolescents at this stage think more logically and abstractly, cognitive features that are more adult-like in nature. They are able to hypothesize and consider possibilities that are not within their realm of direct experience. Early formal operational thinking is often characterized by idealism.

While Piaget's work has given educators a framework to bear in mind when making important decisions about how students think and learn, his theory does have some apparent shortcomings. I believe that if Piaget were to review his cognitive theory today, he would not associate each stage with such specific age parameters. Chronological age does not seem to be a reliable way to assess an individual's level of cognition. His stage theory implies that if a young adolescent has reached age 15, then she is able to think abstractly in all areas. This assumption may not be true. While Amanda may be able to grasp an abstract algebraic concept, she may not be able to grapple with metaphorical thinking in her literature class. Many adults never advance to formal operational thinking in some areas. Finally, the influence of one's culture and exposure to relevant learning experience seems to impact one's pace of intellectual maturity (Cole, 1997). The great variance among young adolescents as to when and to what degree they are able to think at the level of formal operations makes teaching young adolescents especially challenging.

Cognitive theory—Lev Vygotsky

Over the past decade, considerable attention has been given to the work of the Russian developmentalist, Lev Vygotsky, and his view of how youngsters learn. Interestingly, he was born the same year as Piaget (1896) but only lived to be 37 years old. In his short career, Vygotsky proposed several views of cognition that are embraced by many educators today.

Vygotsky believed that one's culture and social contacts significantly impact one's cognitive development (John-Steiner & Mahn, 2003). In his view, knowledge is individually constructed through collaboration with peers and adults. Vygotsky believed that youngsters learn best via interacting with more skilled individuals. One distinctive element of Vygotsky's theory is the *zone of proximal development*. This concept proposes that any type of learning involves an upper and a lower edge of proficiency. At the lower limit, one is able to work independently. But at the upper end of the zone, one needs assistance from a more skilled individual in order to

One's culture and social contacts significantly impact one's cognitive development

progress (Dacey & Kenny, 1997). For example, a young basketball player may learn the basic techniques of shooting a free throw by reading a book and imitating the form of other players. Yet, to become truly proficient, the young athlete will likely need the critique and mentorship of a skilled coach to advance beyond the point at which he is able to learn on his own.

Many present-day educational techniques are grounded in Vygotsky's theory of social cognition. Strategies such as scaffolding, cognitive apprenticeships, cross-age tutoring, cooperative learning, and reciprocal teaching are examples (Santrock, 2005). The popular concept of *constructivist* teaching and learning, a part of the middle school concept, is supported by the theories of both Piaget and Vygotsky.

A time of transition

As is true in every aspect of their lives, the intellectual development of young adolescents is in a state of transition. Stevenson (1998) maintained that misunderstanding of how young adolescents think and learn is the greatest single deficit in practice in most middle schools. Why middle level teachers have traditionally not understood the unique nature of their clientele can be explained partially by examining licensing requirements. For decades, most teachers of young adolescents were prepared to teach at the secondary level, and it was assumed that if one could teach high school students, then middle level students could be adequately served by secondary teachers who could adapt the curriculum and slow the pace of instruction. But young adolescents are not smaller versions of high school students. After reviewing studies concerning intellectual development, Van Hoose, Strahan, and L'Esperance (2001) concluded that only about 33 percent of eighth grade students are able to *consistently* exhibit formal operational thinking. It would be safe to assume that even fewer sixth and seventh graders would be capable of abstract thinking. This means that the vast majority of middle level students still think consistently on a concrete level. Since secondary teachers are trained to work with students who are more adult-like in their cognitive functioning, it is not surprising that there is a disconnect between the curricular demands and the students when high school-prepared teachers are employed to work with middle level students.

Only about 33% of eighth-grade students are able to consistently exhibit formal operational thinking.

One of the seven goals spelled out in *Turning Points 2000: Educating Adolescents in the 21st Century* (Jackson & Davis, 2000) is that middle schools should be staffed with faculty who are experts in teaching young adolescents. This recommendation has frequently and long been made but all too seldom made operational. Many states now respond by requiring middle level teachers to be specifically prepared to teach in middle schools. According to Ference and McDowell (2005), only 25 states offered any kind of middle level certificate or endorsement in the 1980s. Gaskill (2002) reported that 44 states now provide some degree of middle level preparation for teachers who instruct young adolescents; but only 21 states require specific credentials.

Intellectual traits

The middle school philosophy is predicated on the belief that early adolescence is a unique and distinct life stage. Ten- to 15-year-olds are no longer children; neither are they full-fledged adolescents. The intellectual traits discussed below provide examples of how young adolescents think and respond differently from adults and youngsters at other developmental stages.

Attention span. Conventional wisdom maintains that young adolescents have a short attention span and find it difficult to attend to a single topic or task for longer than 15 minutes. And certainly as a general rule, young adolescents do jump from one thing to another quickly; but Findley (2005) warned, "Limited attention span may sometimes be a symptom of teaching that does not connect with children's purposes and interests. Children have an innate desire to understand their world and to accomplish their goals. They can attend for hours to something they understand to be worthwhile and achievable" (p. 653). So before middle level educators attribute inattentive and off-task behavior to low attention span, we should examine the content students are asked to learn and the methods employed.

In order to keep young adolescents focused on the task at hand, effective teachers use a variety of instructional strategies and change the focus of the lesson frequently. Long block scheduling, which provides flexibility in its use, has become common in many middle schools. Teachers who stick to the traditional lecture and worksheet format of instruction render such scheduling deadly for young adolescents. Middle school students dislike lectures and find them boring. While a brief lecture that addresses a few clear points is a legitimate teaching strategy, it must be supplemented with more interactive strategies such as cooperative learning, group projects, simulations, debates, skits, and hands-on projects. These more active and effective teaching strategies require more time to implement, making flexible block scheduling a desired feature of a developmentally responsive middle school.

Idealism. Young adolescents are often idealistic. They regularly have a "perfect vision" of what should be, and they frequently hold exalted views of what parents, teachers, and other adults should be like. The media often contribute to young adolescents' distorted and idealistic views of adulthood by frequently portraying adults in romanticized and unrealistic situations. Young teens may lack the life experiences needed to separate the fantasy portrayed in the media from the reality experienced by almost all adults.

Because of their idealistic thought patterns, anything that is imaginable is possible in the minds of young adolescents. Give them a complex problem and they will devise a relatively simple solution, even though the proposed solution may be impractical. Young adolescents typically can arrive at ways to alleviate homelessness and world hunger overnight. But their idealistic thinking makes it difficult to separate what they think from reality.

Young teens may lack the life experiences needed to separate the fantasy portrayed in the media from the reality experienced by almost all adults.

Idealistic thought also impacts the perspective that young adolescents take on events that they observe or experience. They tend to see events in "black and white" terms. A colleague was chastised by her 13-year-old daughter for proceeding through an intersection on a deserted country road without coming to a complete stop. While a law enforcement officer might have held the same perspective on the situation, the girl demonstrated a young adolescent proclivity to see only black and white, not shades of gray.

Literal. Over the last few years, I have come to realize that young adolescents are very literal when it comes to following directions or complying with something they are asked to do. It is a mistake for adults to assume that young teens will act upon tasks that are simply implied but not explicitly defined. For example, my wife recently asked our 14-year-old son to take the laundry out of the washer and put it in the dryer. He complied. But when my wife returned an hour later to fold the laundry, she found that our son had not started the dryer. Turning on the dryer was not a part of the instructions he was given. Similarly, my son's friend, John, was visiting while my wife was packing for an overnight trip. Several bags had been placed in the trunk of our car which was parked in our garage. My wife asked John if he would carry another bag to the garage for her, which he gladly did. Upon reaching her destination, my wife found that she was missing a bag. She telephoned me to see if I could locate the suitcase. An inspection of the garage revealed the bag sitting on the floor. John had carried the suitcase to the garage as asked, but did not put it in the open trunk of our car as my wife assumed he would.

> Young adolescents are very literal when it comes to following directions or complying with something they are asked to do.

I am not sure why young adolescents are so literal when interpreting instructions. It could be that their cognitive skills have not developed to the point where it is easy and obvious for them to make inferences that are so apparent to adults. Someone theorized that young adolescents are so fearful of "messing up" that they refrain from doing more than what they were specifically told and take all such instructions at face value. Whatever the case, adults need to be aware that young teens seldom read between the lines and take initiative. Asking my son to brush the snow off the windshield of the car does not guarantee that the snow will be removed from the back glass without including that in the original instructions. While requests and instructions to teens need to be detailed and specific, care needs to be taken that they are not delivered in a patronizing or belittling manner.

Seek connections. The brain is a "connection seeking" organ. Every time we encounter a new concept or idea, we try to relate it to something we already know or have experienced. Rick Wormeli (2002) states that, "The pursuit of familiarity is so powerful that the brain will not move anything to long-term memory unless it is connected to something already there" (p. 24). In many middle level schools the curriculum is still organized by separate subjects. Each period students are taught by a subject area specialist with little or no attempt to show how the disciplines are related. Any connections made between what is being learned in English class, for example, and how it relates to current topics being studied in social studies are left for the student to discover. And few middle level students have developed the cognitive ability to make connections among the disciplines unassisted. It is no wonder that young teens often feel that their learning is fragmented and unrelated to anything that resembles reality.

> **"The pursuit of familiarity is so powerful that the brain will not move anything to long-term memory unless it is connected to something already there."**

In more progressive middle level schools, the curriculum is offered via interdisciplinary teams who use themes or units, rather than subjects as a basis for organizing learning experiences. In the purest form of integrative education, students decide which topics or themes are to be investigated. The traditional academic skills and content are mastered, but they are learned as they apply to the theme, rather than being taught in isolation. For example, a team may select "power" as a theme. The teachers and the students on the team then identify and pursue the concept of power in its many meanings. Language arts comes into play as the team addresses the "power of the pen" and persuasive writing is explained. Dictatorships would likely be considered as political power is examined. The power of natural disasters would utilize science, while mathematics would be examined in a unit on exponents—and other areas such as art would also be tapped. This thematic approach will help young adolescents understand how learning and life are interrelated and provide a more meaningful education.

Relevance. Students often ask, "Why do we need to know this?" If the answer given is vague, or if students are simply told they will need to know the information when they get to high school, most students will view the learning at hand as boring or pointless. The vast majority of young adolescents have not developed that love of learning for the sheer satisfaction of conquering an intellectual challenge. But personal relevance is a huge motivator for middle level students. Young adolescents will work hard to master concepts and material that *they* consider to be useful and important to them *now.* In today's climate of testing and accountability, teachers frequently are required to closely adhere to prescriptive curriculum guides and to cover material that will presumably be on mandated, standardized tests. But trying to cram discrete and unrelated facts and information into the heads of young adolescents is really a losing proposition. Many analogies have been used to describe the human brain. While it does absorb, like a sponge, everything it takes in, it quickly lets go of any information that is not directly related to survival or to knowledge already stored in the memory bank, making it a bit more like a sieve than a sponge (Wolfe, 2001). Providing students with opportunities to explore their own questions about themselves and the world in which they live is a sure way to ensure relevance in the curriculum.

Academic decline. Many parents worry about, and teachers are often criticized for, the decline in grades often earned by middle level students. Steinberg and Wheelock (1993) referred to this phenomenon as the "seventh-grade slump," based on the fact that seventh graders often earn lower grades than they did as sixth graders. Many reasons have been suggested for this perceived regression in academic competency—dealing with puberty, a mismatch between the classroom environment and developmental needs of young adolescents, or an overemphasis on performance and achievement rather than learning. Some adults become so frustrated with the poor academic performance of middle level students that they question the logic of trying to educate them at all. I recall hearing one colleague refer to his students as "brain dead."

I urge both parents and teachers of young adolescents not to hit the panic button if the academic records of students regress during the middle school years. Most middle school students are more concerned with their social status than they are with their academic standing—and learning to manage interpersonal relationships, make and keep friends, and fit in with a peer group are extremely important lessons to learn for future success. The problem is that these critical life skills do not show up on standardized tests nor count toward the honor roll. Young adolescents are learning a lot, but it is not always traditional "school stuff." So parents should not worry unduly, and teachers should not put undue pressure on students if their grades slip a bit during the middle school years.

Most middle school students are more concerned with their social status than they are with their academic standing.

With effort and time most young adolescents will return to their previous levels of performance. What does need to be guarded against is students' losing confidence in their abilities. Of course, a sustained academic nosedive should not be ignored since academic failure is often closely correlated with risky and dangerous behaviors.

Argumentative. Young adolescents are often accused of being verbally abrasive and argumentative. The fact is that young teens, due to their more advanced intellectual ability, have become better at arguing. This new-found skill takes some getting used to by the young teen and the adults around him. Young teens may be surprised that they can come up with arguments that can legitimately challenge adult directives. Their task is to learn to present their arguments in ways that are respectful and non-inflammatory. Parents and teachers play major roles in this arena. For adults, it is somewhat unsettling to lose arguments to someone one-third their age. Adults need to refrain from taking comments from teens too personally and avoid power struggles. Middle school advocate Neila Connors often says, "Don't get into an argument with a young adolescent. It is like mud wrestling with a pig. You both will get muddy but only the pig will enjoy it."

Exploration. Early adolescence is a time of exploration. Nearly every facet of their nature predisposes young adolescents to explore new and different elements in their environment. Physically, young adolescents now have the strength and endurance to tackle tasks that were once beyond their capabilities. Socially, they are learning to navigate peer relationships and even dabble in budding romantic interests that were previously unthinkable. Intellectually, young adolescents can understand issues from multiple perspectives and can have empathy toward others in situations that they have not personally experienced. Young adolescents are beginning to consider their *possible selves*—what they aspire to become in the future and what they fear might be their fate. For these reasons, young adolescents should be exposed to as wide a variety of learning experiences and activities as possible so they can discover and nourish their interests and aptitudes.

Introspection. For the first time in their lives, young adolescents have the intellectual ability to turn thoughts inward. Children as individuals are rather unaware of what others think about them or what is their status or social condition. But as young adolescents, they now begin to form impressions of self and how they are perceived by others. Stevenson (1998) states, "Of all the changes taking place during these transitional years, none is more central to a child's growth than the continuously shifting product of introspection: how she perceives herself" (p. 81). During early adolescence individuals form concepts of self that persist into adulthood, thus having long-term impact.

During early adolescence individuals form concepts of self that persist into adulthood, thus having long-term impact.

Perceptive. Young adolescents have keen powers of perception. They are difficult to fool and resent adults who try to do so. As a middle school teacher, I recall having students ask me why the teacher across the hall did not like them. As far as I know, Mr. Green never announced to his students his lack of affection for them, but it did not take long for students to be aware of his true feelings. Students appreciate adults who are genuinely interested in them. Thus, I was delighted during the first week of my son's middle school experience to hear him remark, "Our teachers like us."

Middle school students also are able to distinguish between legitimate homework and busywork. When they view homework as serving no real purpose, motivation to complete it is greatly diminished.

Brain research

One of the most exciting developments in education is the burgeoning level of research on the human brain. Over the last decade, technology has advanced to the point where the brain can now be studied while it is at work. While countless books, workshops, and journal articles have appeared on the topic, experts in the field caution educators not to leap to broad and oversimplified interpretations of this complex field. Teachers should stay current in neurological research pertinent to learning but avoid making one brain theory another educational bandwagon.

While educators should be cautious about faulty interpretation of neurological findings, brain research does give credence to things that middle school teachers have intuitively known for years. Until quite recently, it was thought that brain development was nearly complete by early childhood. That meant the intellectual potential of students was set for life with the cognitive faculty constructed during early childhood. Now we know that the brain continues to develop throughout life, and that there are some critical periods of development. One of those critical periods comes about age 10 or 11 (Franklin, 2005a). At this age the brain undergoes a period of "blooming and pruning" that can have long-term implications for individual students. Giedd and associates (1996) maintained that neurological pathways that are formed and frequently used during adolescence will be strengthened and ingrained while those that are rarely exercised or ignored will be pruned away and lost. This could help explain why habits, values, and dispositions developed during adolescence usually follow an individual into adulthood.

Researchers also have found that the prefrontal cortex of the brain continues to develop and does not mature until near the end of adolescence (Wilson & Horch, 2002). This part of the brain controls organization skills, impulse control, mood modulation, and the ability to objectively evaluate situations and consider consequences of one's actions. Adults who work regularly with young adolescents are often astonished when young teens have difficulty dealing with these abilities. For example, middle school teachers have to devote much time helping students get organized; and parents often field phone calls from their young teens asking them to bring a forgotten band instrument, or lunch, or gym shoes. Middle schoolers are notorious for failing to take rain gear to a soccer match when poor weather is forecast. How can a young adolescent not be surprised that his jump over a makeshift ramp with his bicycle resulted in a trip to the emergency room? The fact that the prefrontal cortex is still under construction goes a long way to explain some actions and behaviors that adults perceive as immature and irresponsible.

Walsh (2004) reported that adults and young adolescents process verbal and nonverbal cues differently. In young adolescents, most impulses are processed directly through the *amygdala*—the part of the brain that controls emotions, including anger and aggression. When a young teen receives a negative message, the amygdala is activated and an angry or aggressive response results. So when a student is bumped in a crowded hallway, he likely interprets the incident as intentional and responds aggressively. Adults, who have built multiple neurological pathways that bypass the amygdala, will understand that a similar incident in a busy airport terminal was an accident and think nothing of it. Walsh explained that young adolescents need adults in their lives to act as a "surrogate prefrontal cortex" since their judgment and ability to respond appropriately are somewhat limited. Adults should advocate for young adolescents by providing guidance, setting clear limits, having reasonable expectations, and allowing young teens to endure the consequences of their actions when those consequences are not dangerous or life threatening. Young adolescents may resent and resist adult monitoring; but, according to Walsh, the payoff comes much later.

The above examples are only a few of the findings that hold promise for teachers to inform their practice. Skillful teachers have always possessed intuitively acquired professional "know how" even when they didn't know how or why things worked. The growing knowledge base about how the brain works can now be used to explain why successful strategies work and point to ways that will ensure a higher level of achievement.

Information processing

Information processing refers to the ways individuals perceive, comprehend, retain, and retrieve information (Dacey & Kenny, 1997). While many mental processes are active in young adolescents, those that follow merit special attention.

Critical thinking. Because critical thinking requires more abstract cognitive ability, young adolescents for the first time in their lives can begin to develop some degree of proficiency in this mental process. Critical thinking requires students to use higher order thinking skills and to delve into advanced levels of Bloom's Taxonomy. Powell (2005) illustrates the complex nature of critical thinking.

> Lipman argues that for students to think critically they
> must be taught, among other things, to change their
> thinking from guessing to estimating, from preferring to
> evaluating, from grouping to classifying, from believing to

assuming, from forming opinions without reasons to offering opinions with reasons, and from making judgments without criteria to making judgments with criteria. (p. 193)

While this implies that critical thinking can be taught, one must question the validity of trying to teach critical thinking skills in the typical teacher-centered classroom. To cultivate students' development of higher levels of thinking it is necessary to engage them in complex problems that require analysis, synthesis, and evaluation. Providing students with learning experiences that require higher order cognitive skills will embed critical thinking in their regular curriculum.

CASE STUDY

IS THIS REALLY AN ISSUE?

One of Sheila's chores at home was to remove empty bottles and cans from the kitchen and place them in the appropriate bins in the garage. After several days, numerous recyclables had accumulated on the counter. Her father reminded Sheila of her neglected duty. Sheila exploded and told her father in an angry tone that she would deal with the refuse when she was good and ready! How should her father respond to Sheila's outburst?

1. Ground Sheila for a week.
2. Take away her allowance that was contingent on her completing her chores in a timely fashion.
3. Take out the recyclables himself to end the confrontation.
4. Leave the bottles and cans on the counter and let Sheila deal with them in her time frame.
5. Let the incident drop for now and speak with her later about more appropriate ways to respond to the situation.
6. Other _____

Comment

It is not uncommon for a seemingly benign comment to elicit a volatile response from young adolescents. Most young adolescents process negative messages through the amygdala, which is the control center for anger and aggression, and they are prone to overreact in anger if they interpret a message to be even the least bit negative. Frequently, young adolescents are surprised and confused by their heated responses. In Sheila's case, it would be wise to have a discussion with her later, after she has cooled down, concerning more appropriate ways she could have responded to the situation.

Decision making. The ability to make good decisions is important to any individual. But for young adolescents, this skill is crucial since many decisions they make have long-term or even lifelong repercussions. As will be discussed in Chapter 8, important choices related to lifestyle, health, and wellness are often made during the middle school years—decisions that were not faced by previous generations until high school or even college.

The model, *The Nine C's of Decision Making* (Mann, Harmoni, & Power, 1989) describe components of good decision making.

- Choice—adolescents make better decisions when they have options and the self-confidence to act on those choices.
- Comprehension—the understanding that good decision making requires logical thought and is a cognitive process.
- Creative problem solving—the ability to identify the problem, generate multiple ways to solve the problem, combine possible solutions to produce new options, select a logical sequence of steps to arrive at the desired outcome.
- Compromise—being able to understand the perspective of others and being willing to negotiate a satisfactory solution for all parties involved.
- Consequentiality—the ability to accurately evaluate the ramifications of one's choices.
- Correctness of choice—the ability to choose the option that will produce the most favorable outcome.
- Credibility—the ability to evaluate the accuracy of information supplied and used to make good decisions.
- Consistency—the ability of an individual to make wise decisions on a regular basis.
- Commitment—the willingness to persist and follow through on decisions made. (p. 265)

Maturity and experience, of course, help young adolescents acquire and hone the elements of making good decisions. Parents and teachers should identify and exploit occasions when youngsters can consciously face, contemplate, and then make decisions.

There are specific instructional practices and strategies that can be used to improve the decision-making ability of young adolescents. Most middle schoolers have trouble visualizing situations they have not personally experienced. For this reason, asking young adolescents to role play realistic scenarios they are likely to encounter is an excellent way to improve their decision-making skills. When youngsters have had an opportunity to process their response to a situation ahead of time, they are more likely to make a good decision when confronted with a similar circumstance in reality. Decision making is a skill. As is true with any skill, practice is needed to become proficient. Allowing young teens to make appropriate decisions for themselves and seeking their input on matters that concern them will give them experience in making decisions. Employing authoritative parenting and teaching practices, as described in Chapter 6, will go a long way toward fostering the positive decision-making skills of young adolescents.

> Allowing young teens to make appropriate decisions for themselves and seeking their input on matters that concern them will give them experience in making decisions.

Creativity. Young children are creative by nature. Observe preschoolers at play and it becomes apparent that their creative juices flow freely. But as youngsters mature, they seem to lose this flair, and by adolescence, many have abandoned individual creativity and action in favor of conformity. The fear of rejection by their peer group and even society in general is so strong that young adolescents tend to forfeit their own individuality in order to fit in.

Educators need to be sensitive to school policies and classroom practices that stifle creative abilities of young adolescents. Truly creative individuals frequently are viewed as a challenge in the classroom. Creative students typically enjoy exploring novel ideas that require them to engage in fantasy and thinking in unconventional ways. Especially in the current age of increased testing and accountability, teachers are tempted to view such out-of-the-box thinking as annoying and a waste of precious instructional time. But inventions and innovations were often developed by individuals frequently viewed as peculiar or eccentric. Thomas Edison was labeled incapable of succeeding in public school. Robert Fulton's sanity was questioned when he proposed putting a steam engine on a boat to mechanically propel it through water. The steam-driven boat was commonly referred to as "Fulton's Folly."

Hallman (1967) outlined a list of "Obstacles and Aids to Creativity" that still serve as wise counsel to educators concerned with encouraging creative thought. He listed the following obstacles to creativity:

- Pressure to conform.
- Ridicule of unusual ideas.
- Excessive drive for success and the rewards associated with success.
- Intolerance of a playful attitude. (p. 325)

Hallman recommended the following practices as ways to encourage creative thinking:

- Encourage self-initiated learning.
- Encourage students to become deeply knowledgeable about subjects of interest.

- Defer judgments—don't give up on novel ideas too quickly.
- Be flexible in one's thinking.
- Ask lots of open-ended questions.
- Learn to cope with disappointment, frustration, and failure. (p. 330)

Implications for middle level curriculum and instruction

Since the middle school concept is based on operating schools in ways that meet students' developmental needs, true middle schools need to reflect those needs in the curriculum and instructional strategies they use with young adolescents. Elements of curricular design and instructional strategies that have proven effective for young adolescent learners are described in subsequent sections.

Middle level curriculum. Critics point out that the middle level curriculum is too "soft and fluffy" and caters more to the social and emotional needs of youth than to challenging them intellectually. No middle level educator need apologize for tending to the affective needs of students, but they should express the view made by Jackson and Davis (2000):

> Let us be clear. The main purpose of middle grades education is to promote young adolescents' intellectual development. It is to enable every student to think creatively, to identify and solve meaningful problems, to communicate and work well with others, and to develop the base of factual knowledge and skills that is the essential foundation for these "higher order" capacities. (pp. 10–11)

In its most recent position statement, *This We Believe: Successful Schools for Young Adolescents*, National Middle School Association (2003) clearly defined the characteristics of an appropriate middle level curriculum. According to NMSA, successful middle schools need to offer a curriculum that is *relevant, challenging, integrative, and exploratory.* Powell (2005) developed the following equations to summarize the four traits of effective middle level curriculum set forth in *This We Believe.*

Relevant Curriculum = Holistic + Personal meaning + New levels of learning

A relevant curriculum addresses issues that involve the cognitive, affective, and psychomotor domains while connecting to the lives and experiences of young adolescents. A relevant curriculum should address current student interests and lead them to a deeper understanding of major and essential concepts. An excellent way to ensure curricular relevance is to allow students to pursue questions they have about topics under study. In some classrooms, students are encouraged to pose questions about issues of personal concern and those of the larger world.

Challenging Curriculum = Substantive + Multileveled
+ Responsibility building

Subject matter content should be substantive. The American Association for the Advancement of Science (Nelson, 2001) endorsed five criteria that should be used to determine the significance of specific content: *Utility*—Will the content be useful in future employment or academic endeavors? *Social responsibility*—Will the content aid the individual in becoming an accountable citizen? *Intrinsic value*—Is there enduring historical or cultural value in the content to be learned? *Philosophical value*—Does the content help learners consider more fully essential questions about life? *Childhood enrichment*—Does the content reinforce the experiences and values learned during childhood?

CASE STUDY

WHO HAS THE QUESTION?

In science class, Ray asked an excellent question that his rookie teacher was unprepared to answer. The question was extremely relevant to the topic at hand and very complex but beyond the teacher's ability to generate a satisfactory reply. How should the teacher respond to Ray's question?

1. The teacher should tell Ray that his question was excellent but he does not know the answer and proceed with the lesson.
2. The teacher should tell Ray to do some research on the topic and report back to the class with his findings.
3. The teacher should tell Ray that he will try to find an answer and get back to him with more information.
4. Other _____

Comment

The best solution seems to be option 3, an option I pursued as a rookie teacher. After spending considerable time researching Ray's question, I did get back to him with a response. His reaction took me by surprise. When I informed him that I thought I had come up with a logical response, he told me that he was no longer interested in the problem. I was stunned and disappointed. But reflecting on the situation, I realized that Ray was upset that I had taken over HIS question. A better response from me would have been to serve as a resource for Ray in his own quest for a solution to the problem he proposed. My eagerness to find the answer to Ray's question stifled his creative thinking and an opportunity to engage him in self-initiated learning.

Such criteria are useful in helping teachers select content that is worthwhile for students to learn. Schools with responsible curricula must be multileveled to meet the needs of diverse learners found in every middle level classroom. The middle school curriculum should also place students in a position where they become increasingly more responsible for their own learning.

Integrative Curriculum = Connections + Sense-making

An integrated approach to curricular design mirrors real life. Every task we undertake every day in the course of living crosses many disciplines. Only in school are learning experiences organized around a single subject. While middle school educators know that an integrated curriculum helps young adolescents find meaning and motivates them at the same time, the pressure for higher test scores and meeting prescribed standards has forced teachers to abandon curriculum integration and embrace a more traditional, subject-specific, teacher-directed approach with focus on teaching, not learning, to deliver the content (Vars, 2001; Weilbacher, 2001). Connections across the curriculum challenge students to critique, analyze, and apply key concepts and skills from every subject. When the curriculum connects for young adolescents, it makes sense to them as well.

Exploratory = Discovery + Choice

Exploring new horizons and expanding boundaries are at the center of being a young adolescent. *This We Believe* (NMSA, p. 23) advises that every aspect of the middle school curriculum should be exploratory in nature. And Powell (2005) noted, "Exploratory, then, does not refer to a set of courses, but rather an attitude and an approach. Discovery and choice are embedded in the disposition that encourages exploration" (p. 152). The middle level is often the last chance for young adolescents to have choices—and to discover what they are interested in. All aspects of the curriculum, and even the entire school day must allow for students to explore widely. A sense of exploration needs to be ingrained in the school's culture as it is in its curriculum.

Instructional strategies. While the developmental traits of young adolescents should be considered when curricular decisions are made, those same characteristics need to be remembered when it is decided how that curriculum will be offered. Some effective middle level strategies, such as interdisciplinary or thematic instruction are embedded in other sections of this text. While many methods of instruction are often effective at any level of education, the following concepts may be of particular importance at the middle level.

Honoring student voice and choice. Young adolescents value adults who listen to them, and they appreciate being heard. At this stage in life they seek increased autonomy. For these reasons, whenever teachers can allow students latitude to pursue legitimate questions of their choosing and provide multiple options for learning, then they are well down the road for making learning relevant and meaningful. One middle level team in Vermont fully embraced the ideals of honoring student voice and choice. The Alpha Team in Shelburne put into full operation the ideas about student-generated curriculum (Kuntz, 2005) 33 years ago. The three teachers on the Alpha Team, a multi-age, 6-8 team, begin the school year with no preset, prescribed curriculum. The entire course of study for the year is constructed around two guiding questions: *What questions and concerns do you have about yourself?* and *What questions and concerns do you have about the world in which you live?* Students spend much time generating responses to those two essential questions. The student questions are then analyzed, consolidated, and refined. Ultimately, consensus themes emerge. Those student-generated themes then become the framework of what they will study for the year.

> Young adolescents value adults who listen to them, and they appreciate being heard.

Another highly successful student-centered program operates at Radnor Middle School in Wayne, Pennsylvania, where two teachers guide 40 eighth-graders as these students determine all aspects of their education (Springer, 2006). In this same school, a comparable seventh-grade program has earned accolades for over 20 years (Springer, 1994).

Teaching in such student-centered classrooms requires a special set of skills and a different mind-set for both students and teacher. The teachers must relinquish much of the control of the learning environment to students. The classroom will buzz with activity, and seldom will all students work on the same task at the same time. The teacher rarely delivers direct instruction to the total class but serves more as a resource person and facilitator for small groups. Teachers in student-generated programs need to be mature, confident, resourceful, and lifelong learners themselves.

While to some, this form of student-directed learning may appear to be chaotic and without structure, nothing is further from the truth. Teachers are still responsible for making sure their students are prepared to meet state standards and the local school district's curriculum guides. But students learn content material and master skills as they pursue learning objectives that they deem worthy. And when it comes to standardized tests, students who have experienced student-generated curriculum did as well or better than their peers who experienced a more traditional form of education (Kuntz, 2005; Alexander, 2006; Springer,

2006). Perhaps most significant is that students in such programs learn how to learn.

Democratic education. The basic goal of education has been debated for decades. Many see schools as a training ground for future careers and the workplace. While preparing young people for the work force is a component of the public schools' mission, others believe schools have a higher calling. Cookson (2001), for example, believes, "Education should not be about producing workers; it should be about educating citizens and developing leaders for the challenges of the future" (p. 42). In his book, *A Reason to Teach: Creating Classrooms of Dignity and Hope*, Beane (2005) has taken the position that the most compelling reason for becoming a teacher is to help students learn the democratic way, which he believes is the most important purpose for schools.

Middle school is the ideal place for students to learn democratic principles. And good middle level teachers embrace the challenge of doing so. Collaborating with students to set academic goals and deciding how those goals can best be accomplished is a valid way to direct the education of middle level students. By implementing what Beane (2002) referred to as the "democratic core curriculum" students learn how questions they have about themselves are intertwined with issues that impact the larger world and come to bear on the common good of all people. By investigating sophisticated questions and working with peers to solve complex problems, young adolescents learn important skills such as building consensus, examining issues from multiple perspectives, and valuing diverse opinions, all of which are important skills in a democracy.

Academic rigor vs. vigor. Politicians and policymakers are clamoring for more *rigor* in our nation's schools. Critics of our educational system often hold up rigor as a virtue to which all schools should aspire. But a reading of my dictionary reveals synonyms such as *harshness, strictness, inflexibility, hardship, severity,* and *oppressiveness.* (Interestingly, the entries directly above and below *rigor* in my dictionary are *rigmarole* and *rigor mortis.*) *Vigor* should characterize effective learning experiences.

The middle school should be the most inviting place in any community. But if education is delivered in ways that are defined as rigorous, it is no wonder that many students dislike school and find routines distasteful. I prefer to use the term *vigor* to describe a learning environment that is more appropriate for young adolescents. The same dictionary cited *strong, healthy, active, energetic,* and *robust* as terms comparable to *vigor.* Surely, any caring adult would strive to educate young adolescents in a vigorous, rather than a rigorous learning environment.

Those who call for middle schools to be more rigorous point to lagging test scores and offer solutions, including more homework, more testing, more time on the basic subjects, reducing exploratories, extending the school day and year, and cutting the frills. Yet, doing more of what schools have always done will not result in a better education.

The problem with using test scores as the primary measure of academic proficiency is that doing well on a traditional examination only requires students to recall stored facts and discrete bits of information. Standardized tests do not require students to comprehend or apply that knowledge. And frequently the content that young adolescents are asked to learn may have meaning and utility in the adult world but is of little relevance to them. The teacher's job goes far beyond transmitting or dispensing information to students. The teacher's role is more a matter of engineering learning experiences and serving as a resource in helping young adolescents find and apply knowledge and solve problems that are of value to them. That bit of educational wisdom, to "start where the child is" is applicable when designing experiences for students. The points of origin should be focused on the personal and social interests of young adolescents since this is "where they are." Learning experiences requiring students to go beyond recall and engage in problems that intersect their lives can be vigorous while meeting real developmental needs.

In summary

Little controversy arose around making middle level schools responsive to the developmental characteristics of young adolescents—until their intellectual development was brought into play. Many middle schools instituted practices that were in line with students' developmental needs but still held to separate subject teaching and textbook coverage that are antithetical to successful middle level schools. Research and best practices have shown us how to better increase learning and academic achievement. But, to do so, educators must be willing to move beyond traditional practices that do not serve today's young adolescents well.

As some young adolescents see it ...

There is a lot more going on in our heads than we let on.
Fred, age 13

I love to learn, but I hate being taught.
Art, age 13

2.
Social Development

Human beings are social creatures, and at no time in their lives are individuals more gregarious than during early adolescence. Around age 10 or 11, children begin to view their friends and peers as the focal point of their lives while parents, teachers, and other previously important adults seemingly fade into the background. The prospect of spending Sunday afternoon at Grandma's is usually met with delight from a seven-year-old. But that same scenario may well bring moans and groans when the youngster is older since the young teen would likely rather spend time with friends than with family. I relish the fact that my son shares my love of athletics. For several summers, we have enjoyed golf outings together. Now that he is 14, he still plays golf with me, but he has a better time if we invite one of his friends to join us; and I know that the day is coming when playing golf with dad likely will lose its luster altogether.

Young adolescents are consumed with their social development. Such questions as *How can I fit in a peer group? How can I be popular and get others to like me? How can I be "cool"? How can I get that boy or girl to notice me?* dominate almost every waking moment for some young people. The social nature of 10- to 15-year-olds can be a source of frustration for adults who work closely with them. For teachers, the primary mission of the school is helping students attain the academic skills and aptitudes necessary to achieve success. However, many middle school students view the role of the school in a very different light. As surveys have shown, the overwhelming majority of adolescents say that the most important reason for going to school is to be with friends. While the academic mission of the middle school will always be a major priority, educators should not try to diminish the importance of the social development of their clientele but rather capitalize on it. The need for social growth and peer affiliation can be used positively in learning activities. Students who find acceptance among their peers are more likely to succeed academically. I am convinced that few academic gains will be made for middle school students until their social and emotional needs are met. Imposing organizational structures and employing instructional strategies that ignore the social needs of young adolescents will yield disappointing results.

Being a parent of a young adolescent, I have struggled with the social aspect of my son's development. I was atypical as a young teen in that I was content to be a "loner." I had friends and peers with whom I associated, and I enjoyed their company; but I do not recall the need to be in frequent contact with or in the presence of friends to the degree that seems to be necessary for my son. My wife, who has always been more extroverted, has been more responsive to Casey's burgeoning social agenda and sees his thirst for peer associations to be more typical of young teens. As a former teacher of young adolescents and now the parent of one, I have labored to overcome my own disposition. I have learned that it is much easier to teach and write about the nature and needs of young adolescents than it is to parent them.

Peer relationships

It is critical for young adolescents to fit in. Belonging to a group satisfies such personal needs as companionship, status, and recognition, and promotes a positive self-esteem and identity. As members of a group, adolescents learn to conduct themselves according to the norms defined by the group and find a specific role to fill. A major reason for having middle schools organized by interdisciplinary teams is to provide young adolescents with an established group to which they can belong. Still largely concrete in their thinking, many young adolescents need visible and tangible signs of affiliation. This is why many middle schools encourage teams to adopt names, mascots, logos, colors, and slogans to help young adolescents identify with their team. Adults, too, frequently display signs of affiliation—bumper stickers in the colors of their favorite team. So the desire for belonging and affiliation is a strong human need.

Finding social acceptance within the peer group is vital for young adolescents. The self-esteem of young teens is closely associated with how they are viewed by their peers. Often they will adopt the speech patterns, dress, and behaviors of the group in order to be accepted. The term "peer pressure" has been coined to describe the phenomenon of allowing real or perceived expectations of the peer group to dictate individual behavior. While peer pressure is not unique to the middle level, it does tend to peak at about age 14.

The self-esteem of young teens is closely associated with how young adolescents are viewed by their peers.

When adults hear the term peer pressure they generally assume the result of it will be devious or detrimental. Adults need to remember that the influence of the peer group can result in positive outcomes as well. If a youngster aligns herself with peer groups that tend to do well academically or refrain from unhealthy or risky behavior, then she will be less vulnerable to negative influences that exist in the culture around her.

While parents and teachers need to be aware that not all peer pressure is negative, the need to conform to peer expectations can be troublesome for young adolescents themselves and can make them vulnerable to making poor choices. Clasen and Brown (1990), suggest the following ideas to help youngsters deal with negative peer pressure:

■ Encourage memberships in and provide opportunities to join groups that encourage positive values such as community service groups, sports teams, scouts, and religious organizations.
■ Permit young adolescents to make choices and to live with the consequences of those decisions.
■ Arm young adolescents with alternatives and ways to resist negative influences.
■ Discuss with young adolescents the potential cost of negative peer pressure.

Negative peer pressure is too complex to be solved by the simple strategy of "Just say no!" In order to consistently make wise decisions in group situations, young teens need to be able to articulate reasons for going against peer expectations and be ready to suggest alternative activities. Teens have little chance of succeeding in this resistance strategy if they have not thought about the possibilities and options ahead of time. Talking with young teens about how they will respond when unwholesome activities are presented by peers and role playing likely scenarios will help youngsters respond in a responsible manner. It is common for young adolescents to resist talking to parents and teachers about sensitive issues. But even if they refuse to engage in conversations about difficult choices, the wheels have been set in motion in their minds concerning how they might respond in such situations. Teens, of course, handle peer pressure better if they have a positive self-image, are self-confident, and have been encouraged to think for themselves. While neither parents nor teachers can inject such positive traits into an individual, they are in a position to engineer situations so that youngsters can make autonomous decisions and develop competencies that will instill confidence and a positive view of self.

Young adolescents also need to realize that going against peer expectations may result in teasing, losing friendships, or being ostracized from the group. But over time, they will understand that good friends will not ask them to do something that goes against their better judgment or violates personal values.

CAN PARENTS MAKE TOUGH DECISIONS?

Your 14-year-old daughter comes home excited because she has been invited to attend a concert by her favorite band with three other friends. The concert will be held in a large city two hours away. When pressed for details, your daughter reveals that the group will be driven to the concert by her best friend's older brother, who is a high school senior. You know your daughter's best friend and she seems to be a mature, level-headed young woman. But you do not know her brother who probably is 17 or 18. As her parent, how would you respond?

1. Allow your daughter to attend and trust her judgment.
2. Call the friend's parents for more details.
3. Investigate the driving record of the brother.
4. Do not allow your daughter to attend the concert.
5. Other _____.

Comment:

Such a situation puts parents in a tough spot but also gives them an opportunity to accept parental responsibilities. Spending time with friends at a concert by a popular band is the epitome of a good time for young adolescents, but the thought of spending four hours on the road with a teenage driver behind the wheel would make most any parents nervous. Few parents would allow a 14-year-old daughter to drive that far with a 17-year-old at the wheel and without close parental supervision for the evening. If the concert were in their own town, it might be appropriate for your daughter to attend, but only with adult supervision.

Multiple versions of self

Adolescents are aware that they exhibit a variety of personas depending on the context or situation in which they find themselves. For example, a young teen is likely to use different language and vocabulary in the presence of his parents than when in the locker room with hockey teammates. He is likely to demonstrate a more refined set of social skills when he is with a girl he wants to impress compared to when he is hanging out with his buddies. Harter, Waters, and Whitesell (1996) used the term *differentiated self* to describe the proclivity of youth to alter their behavior depending on the social context and audience present. This trait is not unique as adults also monitor and alter their behavior depending on the situation and who is within earshot. But young adolescents adapt their version of self as a way to gain social acceptance within the group that they are associated with at any given time.

Independence vs. conformity. Young adolescents are frequently torn between wanting to be distinctive and independent but not wanting to stray too far from peer norms and common expectations. This conundrum often plays out in the selection of clothing worn. In middle schools where all students wear a prescribed school uniform, students often cry foul because the mandatory uniform restricts their individuality or freedom of expression. By spending only a few minutes in the hallways of any middle school, adults would observe that an "unofficial school uniform" does exist—one self-imposed by the students. The fashions in vogue usually are largely dictated by the current celebrities deemed "hot" by young teens. Straying too far from the teen-sanctioned uniform of jeans and T-shirts puts one at risk of taunting and ridicule from peers.

> Young adolescents are frequently torn between wanting to be distinctive and independent but not wanting to stray too far from peer norms and common expectations.

At the same time young adolescents seek autonomy. They want to be viewed as unique individuals. Students whose older siblings precede them through middle school resent teachers who compare them to their older brother or sister. I remember having a mathematics teacher comment to me that she did not understand why I had difficulty mastering a specific algebraic concept since my older sister never experienced any trouble. That comment from the teacher, while not meant to be malicious, troubled me because I was an individual and not a clone of my sister. Anything teachers and parents can do to validate the uniqueness of students will assist them in defining themselves as individuals.

Peer associations

The social world of young adolescents is very complex. During childhood, peers generally include youngsters who live in the same neighborhood, share similar interests, and are of the same sex. But during early adolescence, peer association becomes more heterogeneous; acquaintances now come from a broader geographic area, may represent diverse ethnic and racial backgrounds, and are composed of both males and females.

Since young teens spend most of their waking hours in school, this is where much of the social drama of being a young adolescent is played out as youngsters seek acceptance and membership in a group they admire. So classrooms, cafeteria, and hallways become the sorting fields where middle schoolers assign each other to social groups. Membership in specific groups tends to be based on popularity, social acceptance, and status.

Popularity. Most adolescents long to be among the popular kids in school. Popular adolescents are usually those who are confident but not self-centered, genuinely compliment friends, listen and communicate well with others, come from middle class or affluent homes, are happy and comfortable being themselves, are physically attractive, and intellectually bright (Hartup, 1983; Hollingshead, 1975; Kennedy, 1990; LaFontana & Cillessen, 2002). But this position of popularity presents some pitfalls. Teens who rise to a popular position in a peer group are more prone to cave in to questionable behaviors in order to hold approval from their peers and remain in good standing.

Social acceptance. During the middle school years students tend to assign everyone to specific groups, such as the jocks, nerds, geeks, burnouts, and preppies. The names for these groups vary depending on the times and the geographic region of the country. But the groups tend to be rather universal, each group occupying a distinct rung on the social ladder and in the pecking order. Movement from one group to another is limited and closely governed by specific parameters such as conformity, achievement, and participation.

To gain acceptance into a group, a young teen needs to conform to the group's expectations. Just as interpersonal friendships are built on similar interests and commonalities, the same holds true with group affiliation whose members are bonded by similarity in dress, behavior, values, academic standing, reputation, and socioeconomic status. The best way for an adolescent to be assimilated into a group is to mirror the qualities and behaviors of its members.

> The best way for an adolescent to be assimilated into a group is to mirror the qualities and behaviors of its members.

Adolescents also gain social acceptance through personal achievement. As discussed in Chapter 1, developing competence in any worthy arena is important in constructing a healthy self-concept. Distinguishing oneself as accomplished in a particular field or skill becomes an avenue for peer acceptance and group affiliation.

Students who are popular with their peers generally participate in many school and community activities. Involvement in a number of cocurricular activities as well as community-based sports or clubs ensures that young adolescents will meet other teens with common interests and inclinations.

Status. While social acceptance can be enhanced by conforming to group norms, achieving success, and participating in a variety of activities, the status earned for individuals is assigned by the young adolescents themselves. Adult views of what constitutes worthy achievement and quality activities count for little from the young adolescent's perspective when assigning status to an individual or to a group to which he might belong. For example, if a student were crowned champion of the spelling bee and a classmate won a skateboarding competition, which student would likely receive the highest accolades from his peers? Would the same be true for teachers or other adults?

Athletic competency has long been equated with high social standing for adolescent boys. While the importance of girls' athletics has gained more visibility and acceptance over the last few decades, female recognition and status is still typically earned by forging the "right" interpersonal connections. Receiving an invitation to "hang out" with the popular kids is the best way for young adolescent girls to earn status among their peers.

Cliques. The need for group affiliation and social bonding is so strong that many adolescents link together into small social groups called *cliques.* Cliques generally range in size from three or four to as many as a dozen members. While common interests and similar tastes are often the basis for clique formation, being a member of the same club or athletic team can serve as a catalyst for clique creation. Also, a small group of students who have shared a common experience that set them apart from their peers may form a clique.

While cliques are not inherently bad, they are likely to cause friction among young adolescents. Cliques tend to be exclusive; youngsters who do not fit the membership criteria are not invited to join. For this reason, clique members are frequently viewed as "snobs" by those outside the group. Clique membership is often closely associated with specific attributes and behaviors, some of which may not be positive. Since belonging to a clique requires an individual to conform to group practices and policies, being recognized as a clique member may override personal identity.

Neglected and rejected young adolescents. While most young adolescents find a niche in some specific group, there are always a few who remain socially isolated from their peers. Frequently referred to as *neglected* adolescents, they go through each day hardly noticed or acknowledged by their peers. Neglected students are not disliked by their peers nor do they generally cause trouble. Unfortunately, teachers, too, may overlook these transparent students who are in danger of falling through the systems established to meet their needs.

Rejected students, on the other hand, are frequently disruptive and openly disliked by their peers. Their behavior usually alienates them from classmates and results in their being shunned by others. Teachers generally find it difficult to relate to rejected adolescents since their negative behavior disrupts the learning environment.

Not all students who have difficulty establishing friendships fit neatly into the stereotypes of neglected or rejected students. I remember Jim, an unassuming boy on our sixth-grade team. He came to school regularly, never caused any trouble, but was shunned by his teammates. The reason for his isolation was obvious. Jim wore the same filthy clothes to school every day and had a strong, offensive body odor. When Jim's hygiene did not improve, we referred him to our guidance counselor. She interviewed Jim and learned that his family situation prevented him from coming to school in more presentable fashion. Jim readily accepted an offer from the counselor to use the shower in the boys' locker room and have his clothes laundered at the end of the day. While this intervention did not turn Jim into a social magnet, it did remove a huge barrier that had kept him from earning acceptance from his peers. Assisting neglected and rejected students in developing positive social skills helps them earn status and make friends.

Nonconformity and anti-conformity. While most teens adhere to the norms established by their peers and, to some extent, society in general, a subset of youth culture of nonconformists and anti-conformists exists. According to Santrock (2003), "Nonconformity occurs when individuals know what people around them expect but do not use those expectations to guide behavior. Anticonformity occurs when individuals react counter to a group's expectations and deliberately move away from the actions or beliefs the group advocates" (p. 190). For example, it is common for the national anthem to be played prior to an athletic contest. The protocol for spectators is to stand, face the American flag, remove hats or caps, place one's right hand over the heart, and remain silent or sing along. But a group of nonconformists would remain seated and talk among themselves while the anthem is played, totally ignoring the patriotic ritual. Anti-conformists, on the other hand, would display more "in your face" defiant behavior. They might stand but turn their backs on the flag and raise a clenched fist in protest.

Most adults have trouble understanding teens who conduct themselves in an antagonistic manner. But being noticed and receiving attention is a basic human need, and young adolescents will seek positive attention as long as they can get it. However, if teens remain anonymous and receive no recognition from peers or adults through conventional avenues, they may seek negative attention instead. The worst thing in the world for teens is to receive no attention at all.

Bullying. Not all peer associations are positive and pleasant. While school yards and neighborhood sidewalks have always been infested with bullies, their aggressive and hostile behavior is no longer accepted as a normal part of growing up. Over the last few years, educational journals and professional conferences have been replete with articles and sessions devoted to the problem of bullying in our nation's schools.

Researcher Daniel Olweus (2003), described bullying behavior: "A student is being bullied or victimized when he or she is exposed, repeatedly over time, to negative actions on the part of one or more students" (p. 9). Olweus goes on to say that bullying is a growing menace, becoming more prevalent in many countries around the world. Comparing data from a study he conducted in 1983 and then repeated in 2001, Olweus found the percentage of youngsters falling prey to bullies had increased by 50 percent and the percentage of individuals involved in bullying behavior, either as victims or bullies, had increased by 65 percent.

Between 1983 and 2001 the percentage of youngsters falling prey to bullies had increased by 50 percent and the percentage of individuals involved in bullying behavior, either as victims or bullies, had increased by 65 percent.

Bullying behavior first appears during the elementary school years but peaks in middle school. Bullying at school takes place in locations were adult supervision is minimal, such as restrooms and hallways. While male students have traditionally been characterized as bullies, girls also engage in aggressive behavior although usually more subtle and verbal rather than physical. Girl bullies use strategies such as spreading rumors, telling lies, and excluding or expelling a person from a group.

Technology provides bullies with another avenue through which they can attack others; e-mail, instant messaging, cell phones, answering machines, personal Web sites, and text messages are now all used as means of bullying or harassing others. Studies have found that over half (57%) of young teens report being harassed electronically (Keith & Martin, 2005). The destructive nature of cyber-bullying is enhanced by the speed at which rumors and hurtful slander can be spread. A middle level colleague of mine recently shared how an episode of electronic bullying devastated one of his students and disrupted the entire school. A student had spread a vicious rumor about a peer through her buddy list via instant messaging. The message spread like wildfire. By the next morning, virtually everyone had heard the sordid news—except the victim. The target of the rumor was not aware of her damaged reputation until a classmate asked her if the story was true. She was obviously distraught. But no adults were aware of the turmoil until the young woman confided in a guidance counselor several days later. Parents need to recognize electronic bullying must be combated. No longer is one's home a safe refuge against the neighborhood bully.

Bullying behavior is a major concern for parents and teachers because it has destructive ramifications for both the perpetrator and the injured party. The victim of bullying obviously suffers emotional damage and loss of status in the sight of his peers. Being bullied can cause isolation for the victim as others do not want to be seen with "a loser" or run the risk of being bullied themselves. Bullying victims often are fearful of going to school and may frequently feign illness rather than be subjected to maltreatment. Victims may even carry weapons and resort to violence as a way to even the score against a tormenter. Over time, victims can develop depression and a damaged self-image that can persist for decades.

The bully also may develop some negative attitudes and characteristics that can have long-term ramifications. Bullies frequently acquire a warped sense of control, power, and superiority that may persist in later life.

Which youngsters are likely to be involved in bullying behavior—either as perpetrators or victims? The targets of bullies are often students perceived as vulnerable in some way. Passive, sensitive, and quiet youngsters who have difficulty asserting themselves are frequently singled out for persecution. Overprotective parents may also put youngsters at risk for relentless taunting. Students who exhibit obvious physical or developmental differences compared to their peers or who have their sexual orientation questioned are frequent subjects of bullies. On the other hand, the bullies themselves tend to be individuals who need to feel powerful and have difficulty feeling empathy. They frequently are products of homes where they experienced violence or abuse and have been taught indirectly that aggression is an acceptable way to solve problems.

Bullying behavior needs to be confronted and its prevalence reduced. In recent years, schools have been taken to court because they failed to respond to bullying or the threat of bullying behavior in an appropriate manner. Vermont has recently enacted legislation which defines bullying conduct and requires schools to institute behavior policies to deal with the issues as well as a plan to track complaints. Schools should adopt anti-bullying policies not merely to avoid litigation but rather because it is the morally correct and responsible thing to do (Zirkel, 2003). In an effort to deter bullying behavior, schools have implemented policies and practices such as those provided by the U.S. Department of Education (1998):

- Hold class meetings where teachers and students can discuss or role play ways to respond to bullying behavior.
- Enlist the support of students in defining bullying as unacceptable behavior.
- Involve students in establishing rules for dealing with bullying behavior.

■ Develop strategies with students to ensure they know how to respond when they witness or are directly confronted with the actions
of a bully.

■ Use teaching strategies that encourage positive peer relationships
and collaboration. (p. 24)

The team structure of middle schools should, of course, be used
to the fullest to ensure that every member of the team is treated with
respect and is a valued member of the learning community. Many schools
have incorporated anti-bullying units into their curriculum or have used
school-wide readings and discussions of a common book on the subject
as a way to confront bullying. One young adolescent novel that has been
used for this purpose is *The Revealers* by Doug Wilhelm. The Vermont
author has established a Web site **www.the-revealers.com** devoted to
ideas and resources concerning how the book may be used in an anti-
bullying campaign. McCullen (2001) outlined several sources of online
references and resources that parents, teachers, and students can use.

■ Teaching Tolerance Project—www.splcenter.org/teachingtolerance
■ Bullying.org—www.bullying.org
■ The Anti-Bullying Network—www.antibullying.net
■ Kia-Kaha—www.nobully.org.nz
■ The Center for the Prevention of School Violence—
www.ncsu.edu/cpsv
■ Kidscape—www.kidscape.org.uk/kidscape
■ Bully Beware—www.bullybeware.com/moreinfo.html

It is especially difficult for young adolescents to go against the grain
and do the right thing when doing so puts them out of step with peers.
"The best way to eliminate bullies is to encourage the silent majority to
speak up. The kids, who stand on the sidelines, watching other children
be humiliated, hold the key to reform in their hands. Standing by silently
reaffirms the [bully's] power. Speaking up nullifies it" (Giannetti & Sagarese, 2001, p. 192).

Bullying is a serious issue and its debilitating impact on the victims
and perpetrators alike should not be ignored or trivialized. However,
adults should not overreact by taking every little row between young
adolescents at face value. There is a big difference between teasing and
taunting. Even the best of friends frequently tease each other. While the
words exchanged may sound caustic to an adult bystander, the exchange
can convey a message of acceptance and affection. The line between teasing and taunting is crossed when the intent of the aggressor is to inflict
emotional pain while the recipient is being psychologically dismantled.

Friends. Nothing is dearer to the hearts of young adolescents than friends. Moving to middle school will, in most cases, widen their circle of acquaintances, and the possibility exists that friendships forged in elementary school will be disrupted or evaporate. While the chance of losing long-standing associations may be sad for some, exposure to a larger, more heterogeneous group of peers is exciting. Elementary students, when they anticipate beginning middle school, regularly cite meeting new people and making new friends as the aspect of middle school they most welcome. Young teens long for numerous close associations since one of their social goals focuses on how to relate to and get along with many different kinds of people. Supporting this premise is the fact that middle schoolers desire multiple friends, and the number of friends held by most young adolescents continues to climb until about age 15 (Dacey & Kenny, 1997).

Nothing is dearer to the hearts of young adolescents than friends.

While the friendships among young adolescents are often viewed by adults as fickle and constantly shifting, close personal alliances are actually more stable when compared to those of children. Nevertheless, it is common for childhood friends to drift apart during early adolescence. As youngsters mature the commonality that cemented an earlier friendship may vanish, causing friends to part company. Developing diverging views and attitudes about critical issues that impact them personally or a change in physical or emotional characteristics as youngsters reach puberty can result in friends drifting apart.

Gottman and Parker (1987) outlined six important functions of friends:

- Companionship. Nearly all people desire human contact. But this is especially true of young adolescents who often cite "just hang out" when asked what they do when friends get together.
- Stimulation. Friends can be a source of information or experiences that can motivate youngsters to explore new ventures.
- Physical support. Young adolescents frequently seek the help of friends with all sorts of tasks from homework to chores they are asked to do at home.
- Ego support. Good friends supply reciprocal encouragement and positive feedback to each other.
- Social comparison. Young adolescents constantly worry about how they measure up developmentally when compared to their peers. Close friends provide a human barometer so young teens can frequently gauge how they are doing.
- Intimacy. One of the major differences between childhood and young adolescent friendships is the level of intimacy. Young adolescents value friends in whom they can trust and confide. (pp. 53–57)

Romantic interests. Being a young adolescent leads individuals into many new and uncertain situations. None of the special experiences of this age group is more mysterious than the romantic stirrings that young teens feel toward another individual. During early childhood little attention was paid to the gender of sandbox friends. In elementary school, members of the opposite sex are generally held in contempt and shunned. But as early adolescence sets in, attitudes and feelings about the opposite sex begin to change. Surveying sixth graders, Buhrmester (2001) found that 40 percent admitted that they "liked someone." No longer do boys claim it to be "cruel and unusual punishment" to have to sit by a girl in science class. Similarly, girls in middle school frequently find the boys, who were the bane of their existence in earlier grades, are now strangely fascinating.

Young adolescent dating. For young adolescents today, "going out with someone" generally means a couple has acknowledged a mutual attraction for each other. Frequently, this acknowledgment is sought via a note written by the admirer delivered through a third party or by sending a friend on a scouting mission to investigate the feasibility of a budding relationship. If the mutual attraction is confirmed, the couple may spend short periods of time together, eat lunch with a shared group of friends, and talk on the phone or online. Young adolescent couples frequently ask adults to drive them to a shopping mall or go to a movie with a mixed group of friends as a way to explore romantic relationships.

The dating process generally evolves throughout adolescence and into early adulthood and usually culminates in mate selection. But for the young adolescent, "dating" fulfills several personal needs. First of all, dating provides recreation—something to do. It also serves as a litmus test for young teens to determine how attractive they are to others. By dating, youngsters begin to sort out the qualities that they value in others; they also learn social skills that are appreciated by members of the opposite sex. The self-esteem and status of a young teen can often be enhanced by the quality of a romantic relationship he or she establishes. Since parents have little control over the selection of their child's dating partner, young teens gain a sense of autonomy by dating. The dating experience for middle school students is rather self-centered and never seen as the beginning of a lasting relationship. Many middle school boys are not even aware that they are "going steady" until they are told by their more mature female friends.

Because of societal changes and more permissive parenting, the age at which American youngsters begin dating has dropped over the last several decades. In the 1920s, the median age for girls to have their first date was 16. By the mid-1990s that same statistic had fallen to 13 years

(Rice, 1996). Young adolescents should be guided and monitored during this pivotal period since early dating has been closely associated with teen pregnancy as well as difficulty at school and home (Santrock, 2005).

Dating protocols. In previous generations males took the lead in asking for and initiating social relationships. Girls were more passive and waited for "him" to call; but girls today are much more proactive in pursuing male attention and companionship than was the case in the 1960s and before. The new order does present some role reversals. Boys have to learn how to tactfully refuse unwanted attention while female suitors need to deal with the possibility of rejection.

Online dating. Cyber-dating, or meeting and establishing romantic relationships over the Internet, has become very popular among middle level students. Technology has opened a multitude of opportunities for young adolescents to meet new people. Unfortunately, sexual predators peruse Web sites and chat rooms looking for easy prey. For this reason, parents and teachers need to counsel young teens to never give out personal information to unknown individuals and to monitor their online activities. A teen should never agree to a face-to-face meeting with an individual whom she met on the Internet without intense scrutiny and close supervision from parents or other adults invested in a youngster's well-being.

Sexual orientation and sexual identity. Just growing up is a challenge for most young adolescents, but young teens who discover that they are gay or lesbian have an additional set of difficult social and emotional hurdles to negotiate.

The issue of sexual identity is of particular importance to middle level educators and parents, because during these years most sexual minority individuals begin to recognize their uniqueness. In a study of gay adolescent males, Newman and Muzzonigro (1993) found the average age when their subjects realized they were gay was age 12.5 years. Many of the boys in the study reported they felt confused and tried to hide the fact they were gay. In another study, young gay males reported having fewer friends and smaller social networks compared to their heterosexual peers. Gay adolescents also reported more anxiety associated with losing friends and not being in control of romantic relationships (Diamond & Lucas, 2004).

National Middle School Association (2003) in its position paper, *This We Believe: Successful Schools for Young Adolescents,* called for middle schools to create an "inviting, supportive, and safe environment" (p. 12). This supportive community is characterized by an absence of "harassment, verbal abuse, bullying, and name-calling" (p. 13) and is essential for all students regardless of their possible uniqueness.

Implications for teachers. Most educators believe that educational gains can best be made by meeting students at their points of developmental readiness. For young adolescents, this means that they are motivated by whatever advances their social agenda. Wise middle level educators pay attention to the developmental traits of their students and use those characteristics to guide policies and practices they employ with students. To that end, Hicks (1997) provided the following questions for educators to consider when evaluating their practices against the social needs of young adolescents and making the curriculum and learning atmosphere developmentally responsive:

- Are there unnecessary policies and practices in this school that force students to choose between their academic work and their friends?
- Are there ways we could allow more social interaction, at little cost to school safety or academic progress?
- Why is student silence the yardstick by which we so often measure the quality of a school or classroom?
- How can we help students monitor and regulate their social interactions for themselves, rather than imposing control by authorities?
- Are there tasks in my curriculum that could be dealt with as group projects, rather than individual ones?
- How can I guide students to work together in a way that is socially satisfying, while still being academically worthwhile?
- Are there ways that students can help formulate rules or expectations for one another that will encourage responsibility and relatedness simultaneously?
- Who are the popular kids in our school and how did they get popular?
- What legitimate ways are there for students in this school to gain visibility and recognition? (p. 21)

In summary

For decades, middle level advocates have championed the cause of educating the whole child. They hold fast to the concept of nurturing the entire being of students. But the idea that schools should be about primarily if not completely filling students' minds with facts and information deemed important by adults and publishers of standardized tests has been a hard nut to crack. Many who oppose the middle school concept seem to believe that providing a rigorous curriculum and attending to the other developmental needs of young adolescents are mutually exclusive. Critics of middle schools trot out the same old, unsubstantiated stereotype—that middle schools do not attend to academic achievement, focusing instead on social and emotional development. While still pervasive, this stereotype has not been proven to be true. More important, it misses the mark by a mile.

Why can't young adolescents have both—a curriculum that is vigorous and relevant to their lives *and* a learning environment in which their affective needs are met? In fact, it is not an either-or proposition; for as pointed out in *This We Believe,* in a true middle school, one that embraces and employs the middle school philosophy wholeheartedly, students will learn to learn, perform well academically, and enjoy an appropriate environment that supports their total growth and development.

As some young adolescents see it ...

Because I am concerned about what my friends might think, I am afraid to be myself.
Rachel, age 14

Peer pressure has caused me to do things my parents wouldn't want me to do.
Ethan, age 13

Don't worry about being popular. I am super weird and I have lots of friends.
Sam, age 14

Some peer pressure is good. My friends all get good grades. If I don't they might look down on me so this helps me keep my grades up.
Kendra, age 13

To be cool at my school you have to be funny, wear the right clothes, and, of course, you have to be pretty.
Marcie, age 14

3.
Physical Development

There may be nothing more complex than trying to understand and explain human nature. While the intellectual, social, physical, emotional, and moral domains of development are presented in separate chapters of this book, these domains do not operate in isolation from each other in the lives of adolescents—far from it. These areas of development intersect and interact routinely for young adolescents, making for complex issues and problems with which they must deal every day. For example, acne is the bane of many young adolescents. But pimples, a phenomenon of the physical domain, are of little importance when at home. They do, however, take on great significance if a young adolescent is to be seen in public, especially by his or her peers. Likewise, the young adolescent girl who has a birthmark on her shoulder is not concerned about its presence until she goes to the beach. In both cases, the physical domain is of little consequence until the social and emotional domains are interwoven.

While a host of developmental changes are taking place with young adolescents, the physical changes taking place within their bodies receive much attention. This focus on physical transformation is largely due to the fact that many of the changes are so obvious—to the young person and to others. Often these dramatic changes are explained by one word—puberty. This word often evokes a feeling of fear and dread in adults who work with young teens. Yet no adult has ever emerged from adolescence without navigating the biological phenomenon of puberty. Puberty is a period of rapid physical maturation involving hormonal and bodily changes, including sexual maturation.

Hormonal changes and puberty

During childhood, the endocrine system of the human body has been dormant or operating in slow motion. But, at the onset of puberty, the endocrine system becomes fully engaged and active. Chief among the endocrine glands is the *pituitary*, a small organ about the size of a garden pea situated at the base of the brain. Not only does this gland influence body growth but it also works in conjunction with the *hypothalamus*, also located in the brain, to control all other endocrine organs. Because of its regulator function over the other endocrine organs, the pituitary frequently is referred to as the master gland.

During early adolescence, the pituitary gland produces several hormones that are secreted directly into the bloodstream. These hormones stimulate other specific endocrine glands, primarily the thyroid, adrenal, and gonads, which bring about many physical changes associated with puberty. Hormones from the pituitary stimulate the *thyroid gland*, located in the throat, to produce hormones that are responsible for physical growth. Both skeletal and muscular growth and maturation are largely controlled by the function of the thyroid.

While less is known about the specific function of the *adrenal glands*, it is thought that these organs do play a key role in the physical development and behavior of adolescents, especially boys. The adrenal glands sit like caps atop each kidney. The adrenal glands manufacture adrenaline, a hormone that enables quick surges of energy and strength, especially during an emergency. As is common of other endocrine glands, it takes some time for the endocrine system to stabilize itself and operate smoothly. It is common for young adolescents to receive huge adrenalin surges for no apparent reason, an unfortunate occurrence when seated in a quiet classroom and unable to respond to the urge to run, jump, or shout.

Finally, the *gonads* or sex glands are stimulated by the pituitary to create the sexual traits of the maturing male and female. Again, under the influence of the pituitary gland and hypothalamus, the male gonads or *testes* produce sperm, the male reproductive cells. The testes also produce testosterone, a hormone that regulates male secondary sex characteristics such as voice changes, body and pubic hair growth, and appearance of a beard. In females, the gonads are called *ovaries* and produce egg cells. The ovaries also produce a hormone called estradiol, which is responsible for the physical changes typical of the more mature female form such as breast development and a widening of the hips.

Timing of puberty and order of physical changes

Young adolescents are good observers, keenly aware of the physical changes they notice in themselves and their peers. Often young adolescents will pose the question, usually to themselves, "Am I normal?" This is especially true if young teens see themselves on either end of the developmental spectrum. Early-developing adolescents will often go to great lengths to hide their maturing bodies while late-developing youngsters often doubt that they will ever "catch up." Although chronological age is a poor marker for puberty, this biological event is likely to occur as early as nine years of age or as late as age 16. Both ends of the spectrum are within the range of normal physical development. For boys, growth in height may occur into the early 20s.

Young adolescents are good observers, keenly aware of the physical changes they notice in themselves and their peers.

Even though the onset and duration of puberty is difficult to predict, there are some physical developmental features that tend to mark its progression. Following is the sequence of developmental changes that occur for young adolescent males and females:

Sequence of Physical Changes for Young Adolescent Males

- Genitals increase in size
- Appearance of straight and fine pubic hair
- Minor voice change
- First ejaculation
- Pubic hair becomes more coarse
- Major growth spurt
- Growth of body hair
- Major voice change
- Growth of facial hair

Sequence of Physical Changes for Young Adolescent Females

- Breast development
- Appearance of pubic hair
- Axillary (armpit) and body hair appears
- Major growth spurt
- Hips widen—become broader than the shoulders
- First menstruation (Santrock, 2005, p. 88)

The sequence of the physical changes ushered in by puberty as listed above is very stable, although the rate varies widely. Individual rates of development can weigh heavily on the minds of young adolescents. Young adolescents need to be reassured that their individual timetable for development is correct for them and that they will emerge from adolescence as a fully developed adult.

The sequence of the physical changes ushered in by puberty is very stable, although the rate varies widely.

Factors that influence the onset of puberty

While the exact onset of puberty is difficult to predict for an individual, there are some factors that tend to influence its arrival. Heredity is a major factor. If one's parents developed early or late there is a good chance that their offspring will follow a similar developmental course. One's race is another condition that influences the timing of puberty. African American children tend to reach sexual maturity earlier than their Caucasian counterparts. Environmental influences such as nutrition also play a role in the timing of puberty. It used to be thought that eating a healthy diet would enhance physical development. While good nutrition is beneficial and healthy, recent studies have indicated that youngsters from economically deprived families, who typically lack proper nutrition, often develop early (Herman-Giddens, Slora, & Wasserman, 1997). Obese children often mature early (Kaplowitz, Slora, Wassermann, Pedlow, & Herman-Giddens, 2001). This observation is associated with the reality that the beginning of menarche is coupled with attaining a specific body weight. With today's youth eating high calorie diets and leading more sedentary lives, many young adolescents are reaching the weight threshold at an earlier age, thus triggering puberty. Adequate health care, or the lack thereof, can also have an accelerating or delaying effect on the onset of puberty. Even emotional stress can have a detrimental effect on physical maturation.

Sexual maturation. Embedded in puberty is the phenomenon of sexual maturation, the point at which a young teen has developed the biological potential to reproduce. For a young adolescent girl, her first menstrual period, known as menarche, is the signal that she has crossed the threshold into womanhood. While the average age for girls to experience their first period has decreased significantly over the last century and huge individual variations in timing exist, most girls experience their first menstruation between ages 12 and 13 (Stevenson, 1998). Some evidence suggests that specific biological parameters must be attained before menarche will occur. For example, Friesch (1984) found that girls weighing about 106 pounds would soon experience their first period. Others have theorized that 17 percent body fat, coupled with the total body weight parameter, is an indicator of impending menses. While neither view has been consistently verified by recent research, there does seem to be some validity to the theory. Adolescent girls and women who go on strict diets or are under stringent physical training regimens and lose a substantial percentage of body fat will often stop menstruating, a condition called amenorrhea. This disruption in the menstrual cycle demonstrates a link between the ratio of body fat to total body weight and menses.

For young adolescent males, there is no analogous event to mark the beginning of manhood. But a boy's first ejaculation of semen, known as spermarche, is a sign that childhood is coming to an end. This event usually occurs at night with an involuntary expulsion of semen called a nocturnal emission or "wet dream." The ejaculation also can occur during masturbation.

Just as is the case with adolescent girls who need to possess accurate information about menstruation, young males need to know that nocturnal emissions are a normal part of growing up. To experience these biological rites of passage without being knowledgeable of what is happening can be very unsettling for unprepared adolescents. Manning and Bucher (2001) reported that 88 percent of girls and 83 percent of boys reach puberty by age 14. This ensures that the vast majority of students will experience sexual maturation during their middle school years. Parents and teachers of young adolescents need to make sure that young teens are armed with factual information to help them negotiate the confusing processes of normal human growth and development.

Growth spurt and asynchronous development. During childhood both boys and girls experience a steady but relatively slow pattern of physical growth. But, coupled with puberty, young adolescents go through an intense period of rapid growth that quickly transforms the body into more adult-like proportions. Girls typically begin their growth spurt about two years ahead of boys, starting around ages 10 to 12. Boys, on the other hand, begin their stage of rapid growth between the ages of 12 and 14. This means that the average girl is generally taller and larger than the average boy at the middle school level. By high school, most boys have caught up and surpassed most girls in height, weight, and physical strength. Most young adolescents grow between two and four inches in height annually and gain between eight and ten pounds during the middle school years.

It is possible for some students, over the course of their middle school career, to grow as much as ten

Most young adolescents grow between two and four inches in height annually and gain between eight and ten pounds during the middle school years.

inches and gain nearly 50 pounds (Van Hoose, Strahan, & L'Esperance, 2001). For an adult, such an increase in body mass over a relatively short period of time would suggest a medical emergency. But for young adolescents, such growth is normal.

CASE
STUDY

DEFIANCE OR HORMONES?

Ms. Hernandez, an eighth-grade mathematics teacher, asked Sam to go to the board and demonstrate a solution to a homework problem. Sam refused to leave his seat. She was a bit surprised by his refusal to comply with her request since Sam was typically quick to respond. Ms. Hernandez pressed Sam a bit more forcefully, and he responded in a sharp tone that he was not going to the board and she could not make him. What should Ms. Hernandez do?

1. Ignore Sam's outburst and proceed with the class.
2. Send Sam to the office for rude and inappropriate behavior.
3. Insist that Sam work the problem and not proceed until he had done so.
4. Ask Sam to stay after class to talk with Ms. Hernandez.
5. Other _____

Comment:

A number of things could evoke a response similar to Sam's. Regardless of the situation, it is never a good idea to engage a student in a power struggle, especially if other students are present. In evaluating Sam's response, one possible explanation could be that he was experiencing a spontaneous erection. Young males frequently experience such occurrences. He may have been concerned that his classmates would notice his aroused condition if he complied with Ms. Hernandez's request to work at the board. A good policy would be to allow students to pass if they are not comfortable performing in front of the entire class, for whatever reason. Then encourage reluctant students to take more active roles in class as the term progresses.

It is crucial that young adolescents understand what is happening to them during periods of rapid growth. One of the problems with adolescent growth is that body parts do not develop at the same rate. Usually the extremities grow faster than the body. Arms and legs, feet and hands may appear out of proportion with the rest of the torso, giving the individual a gangly appearance. Not only does such rapid growth cause a change in appearance but frequently results in a loss of coordination. Youngsters often experience a decrease in fine motor control, making handwriting more laborious. This could be one reason why many middle school students complain about having to take notes and complete lengthy handwriting assignments. The regression in fine motor skills also results in objects being accidentally dropped or stumbling for no apparent reason. Young adolescents often feel that their body has betrayed them, since many physical tasks that they could previously perform flaw-lessly are now a chore to accomplish.

Young adolescents need to be armed with factual information about the "awkward stage" that many must endure. They need to be reassured by parents and teachers that as they grow accustomed to their new size and shape that their coordination and physical prowess will not only return but with more adult-like precision, strength, and stamina.

Skeletal and muscular development. The majority of the body's skeletal and muscular development occurs during adolescence. During periods of rapid growth, skeletal development outpaces muscular growth. Because the bones grow faster than muscles, many bones of the body are not protected by large sheets of muscle as they are in older adolescents and adults, making the young adolescent more prone to fractures. Also, since the long bones of the body are still growing and the growth cartilage at the ends of bones is softer and weaker than a fully developed bone, they are more prone to injury. The prevalence of casts, splints, and crutches worn by middle level students is evidence that injuries to bones, muscles, and joints are common.

Overuse and repetitive motion also can tax the developing body and cause severe or even permanent damage to joints, muscles, ten-dons, ligaments, and bones. Swaim and McEwin (1997) reported that nearly one-third of all sports-related injuries in the United States occur to children and young adolescents between the ages of five and 14 and that a high percentage of those injuries take place during school-spon-sored games or practices. With the increase in the number of organized sports opportunities for children and young adolescents in the last few decades, incidents of sports-related overuse injuries have become com-mon. Generations ago, when youngsters were left alone to organize their own games on the sandlot, overuse injuries seldom occurred. When kids got tired they simply stopped playing. For this reason, caution should be exercised by physical education teachers, athletic coaches, and sports camp directors in making sure that condition-ing, practice, and game procedures are appropri- **Incidents of sports-related overuse** ate for the budding young adolescent athlete. **injuries have become common.** National Middle School Association (1997, *Research Summary #10: Sports in the Middle Grades*) questioned the ap-propriateness of competitive, interscholastic sports at the middle level. With athletics engrained as an icon in the American culture, it is difficult to imagine many middle schools backing away from interscholastic ath-letics and replacing them with less structured intramural sports programs. But adults in charge of middle level cocurricular activities should work to make sure that athletic programs are organized and operated with the best interests of young adolescents in mind. A report (University of Maine, 2005) entitled *Sports Done Right* provides many excellent examples and suggestions for appropriate middle level sports.

UNREALISTIC COMPETITION?

For several years, Alexander Middle School has sponsored a seventh- and eighth-grade football team. The middle school coaches routinely have had similar philosophies and frequently collaborated about coaching philosophy, playing time, and strategy. Over the years they never allowed the seventh- and eighth-grade teams to scrimmage each other, but one year the very successful seventh-grade team challenged the eighth-grade team to a scrimmage. You are a member of the coaching staff. What position do you take?

1. Endorse the scrimmage in the name of friendly competition.
2. Tell the students that they could have their scrimmage but the coaches could not endorse it.
3. Use the scrimmage as a regular practice for both teams.
4. Talk with the players about why the scrimmage is not appropriate
5. Other _____

Comment

Many middle level experts and National Middle School Association question the appropriateness of contact sports for young adolescents (Swaim & McEwin, 1997). But if middle schools do sponsor such activities, the safety of the athletes must take top priority. It is assumed that the coaching staff never practiced the seventh and eighth-grade teams together for safety reasons. There are huge physical differences between most seventh- and eighth-grade boys. The potential physical mismatch is reason enough to veto the scrimmage. The coaches should stick to their policy of not having these two age groups compete against each other but explain their policy and the dramatic differences in growth and development that underlie it.

Ossification. Other changes in the maturing skeleton of young adolescents also occur. During childhood the last three vertebrae are separate and individual bones. During adolescence, these three bones fuse together to form the adult coccyx or tailbone. During this process of ossification, or fusing of the vertebra, the tailbone may become tender or sore, making it uncomfortable to sit in one position, especially on hard surfaces, for any length of time. This is one reason why young adolescents need to—and do—change positions frequently and are often fidgety.

DOES ONE SIZE FIT ALL?

Your request for new classroom furniture has finally been approved by your principal. Over the course of a year you have noticed that several seventh-grade students no longer fit well into the student chairs you currently have in your classroom. What factors should you consider in requisitioning new furniture to accommodate the vast physical diversity represented by the young adolescents in your classes?

1. Order chairs that are large enough to accommodate any size student.
2. Request student chairs in a variety of sizes so each student can select furniture that would best fit him or her.
3. Consider furniture that will facilitate the type of learning activities that you offer your students, possibly tables and chairs.
4. Other _____

Comment

In our adult wisdom, it seems logical to have furniture in our classrooms that would accommodate the wide range of body types represented in most middle school classrooms. But from the perspective of young adolescents, students that deviate from the average size of their peers might feel self-conscious about having to sit in a chair that accentuates their differences. Employing teaching strategies that allow student frequent student movement minimizes the problem. Also, allowing students to adopt unusual but safe sitting postures is an alternative. Consider permitting students to stand or sit on the floor for a period of time, as long as they are engaged in the learning at hand. This is being responsive to their developmental needs. The use of tables and chairs rather than individual student desks seems to accommodate middle school methods.

Puberty and other biological functions

Puberty, and the rapid growth associated with it, impacts other organs and systems of the body. The heart increases in weight and the lungs increase in size, giving the growing adolescent more stamina. The stomach, too, becomes more elongated and increases in capacity. The skin undergoes a dramatic change during puberty as well. Sebaceous or oil glands become more active during puberty, secreting oil into the pores of the skin. Occasionally the oil, along with dead skin, will clog the pore and a minor infection will result in a pimple. Multiply this condition several times and a young teen has developed a case of acne. The commonly held beliefs of previous generations that acne was caused or worsened by certain foods or sexual activity are unfounded. Even the eyes undergo changes due to body growth. As many as 25 percent of young adolescents experience nearsightedness or myopia, an inability to focus properly on distant objects, but can see clearly things that are at close range (Gilmartin, 2004). This condition is caused by the eyeball being elongated, resulting in light being focused in front of the retina and producing a blurred image of objects far away and can be corrected with prescription glasses or contact lenses. Many parents also claim an acute decline in the auditory ability of their children, noticing that their hearing becomes quite selective; but no scientific evidence supports that observation.

Nutrition. It takes a lot of energy to sustain energetic young adolescents and to support their enormous physical growth. The fuel is furnished by the calories contained in the food adolescents eat every day. While active and growing teens require more calories than at any other point in their lives, the source of those calories is critical to support good health and proper development. It is well known that many young adolescents make poor choices when it comes to their diets. Foods that are high in fat and sugar, contain empty calories, and are devoid of essential nutrients dominate the diets of many young teens. Research indicates that the majority of young people eat too much fat and only 20 percent consume the recommended allotment of five servings of fruits and vegetables per day. Calcium intake, which is essential for proper bone development and important in warding off osteoporosis later in life, is generally insufficient. One in five young adolescents typically skips breakfast, arguably the most important meal of the day (Centers for Chronic Disease Prevention, 2002).

The majority of young people eat too much fat and only 20 percent consume the recommended allotment of five servings of fruits and vegetables per day.

Not only is poor nutrition a health concern for developing young adolescents, but all too often the eating habits established during adolescence follow individuals into adulthood. Obesity among adolescents for example, an issue that will be discussed later, is a growing concern for health care providers. Research by Engeland, Bjorge, Tverdad, & Sogaard (2004) indicated that poor eating patterns developed during childhood and adolescence were highly correlated with obesity in adulthood. Conklin, Marshak, and Meyer (2004) corroborated the above finding by stating, "Choices lead to behaviors, behaviors lead to habits, and habits lead to a way of life. Today, the health of young adolescents and the adults they will become is critically linked to the health-related behaviors they choose to adopt." Research by Young and Fors (2001) found that youngsters make better dietary choices when their eating is monitored by parents. Therefore, eating is not an area that should be totally left to the discretion of young adolescents. Adults should see that young adolescents have ample, healthy choices in their diets.

"The health of young adolescents and the adults they will become is critically linked to the health related behaviors they choose to adopt."

Hygiene. As young adolescents reach puberty, more care needs to be exercised about cleanliness and personal hygiene. The sweat glands of young teens become more active than they were during childhood. While perspiration is odorless, the sweat glands concentrated under the arms, in the groin, and on the feet help to create a warm and moist environment for odor-causing bacteria to grow. Young adolescents, therefore, will find that they need to shower or bathe more frequently, apply underarm deodorant, and change clothes daily, especially socks and underwear, to keep from developing offensive body odor. Maturing girls also require counsel around personal care associated with the onset of menarche.

Sexuality. Children are well aware that there are physical differences between their male and female peers. From a child's perspective those differences are subtle and vague, but as the youngster enters puberty, he or she becomes keenly aware of the biological differences between himself or herself and members of the opposite sex. Curiosity about sexuality often dominates the thoughts of young adolescents. Teachers of middle level students know this to be true.

A part of growing up is becoming a sexual being. Having romantic interests in another person is normal and natural. While this new interest can be very exciting, it can also be confusing. For a young boy, having to sit or stand beside a girl could be mortifying. But as a young adolescent, the same prospect often loses its dread. For elementary school girls, male peers are usually viewed as "public enemy number one." But those same boys become more tolerable and even interesting as they mature.

Once the mysterious nature of the opposite sex subsides, young adolescents begin to focus their attention and affection on specific individuals. It is very common for initial romantic experiences to be brief as young teens learn that there is more to a relationship than physical attraction. As a middle school teacher, I recall one eighth-grade male having three different "girlfriends" on a daylong field trip to a major city. He boarded the bus with girlfriend number one, a young woman he had "gone with" for a couple of weeks. But on the five-hour ride to our destination, they discovered they really had little in common and "broke up." While at our destination, I observed this same young man strolling hand in hand with a new friend. But by the time we left for home, the couple had a "falling out" and the young man found another female companion to share a seat on the bus ride home. Such is the fickle nature of young adolescents. Yet, such experiences are important for young teens as they begin to sort out the traits and characteristics they appreciate and value in a person with whom they would eventually wish to have a long-term relationship.

Many young adolescents have their first boyfriend or girlfriend during the middle school years with romantic feelings and affections focused on one individual. But by eighth grade, boys and girls have developed a different attitude about sex and romantic experiences. According to Stevenson (1998), girls usually have a romanticized and idealized view of relationships with boys. Often their relationships are like those portrayed in the novels they read or presented in the media. Also, girls who have a boyfriend usually are afforded higher status among their peers. Boys, on the other hand, generally have a more carnal interest in their relationship with girls and are more interested in experiencing some physical intimacy firsthand. Fortunately, few boys are bold enough to act on these instincts.

Young adolescents should not be made to feel guilty or perverted for having sexual feelings. But young teens need to be cautioned about the physical and psychological dangers of acting on those feelings. While most young teens may be biologically equipped to have sexual intercourse, rarely is a teenager ready to deal with the emotional aspects and responsibility of an intimate physical relationship. Adolescents who have boyfriends or girlfriends should explore other aspects of their relationship. Enjoying mutually interesting activities, developing a true friendship, and "comparing notes" on what is being learned about life in general are positive ways to spend time together. Sex should be saved for the right person and at the right time.

Sometimes young teens find that they are attracted to individuals of the same sex. This does not necessarily mean that they are homosexual. But such feelings can be confusing. As teens learn more about their developing sexuality, some realize that they are gay. While attitudes about sexual orientation are changing, prejudice, discrimination, and even persecution of gay and lesbian individuals is still a reality. It is important for young adolescents who have questions about their sexual orientation and identity to find help and support. Talking with a trusted adult or accessing a reputable support group would be in order.

Psychological implications of puberty

At a public beach a young boy was playing in the sand without wearing a stitch of clothing. He was oblivious to the fact that he was the only nude person on the beach and was not at all concerned that others could see his naked body. This episode illustrated a major cognitive difference between children and adolescents and an example of how the domains of development for teens intersect. Young adolescents are keenly aware of their appearance and how others perceive them while children are not.

Body image is usually a major concern for young adolescents. Their preoccupation with their appearance is evident by their frequent need to inspect their image in a mirror. Some middle schools accommodate this need of young adolescents by strategically placing mirrors in classrooms—a practice that results in a decline in requests for restroom passes. Girls frequently place a mirror on their locker door. Since physical appearance is often a basis for peer selection, social image, and romantic appeal, all important issues to young adolescents, it is not surprising that they give much attention to this issue. Self-esteem is also closely linked with how satisfied young adolescents are with their personal appearance.

Both middle school boys and girls pay close attention to their general appearance, facial features, complexion, hair, and body build. Hair especially receives much scrutiny and frequent styling since this is one aspect of appearance that young adolescents feel is within their control. Body shape is also a huge concern to all young teens, but especially girls. Our society portrays the lean and athletic shape as the form of preference, and many young adolescents go to great lengths to look like the models and stars featured in the media. Since many, if not most, youngsters are not happy with their pubescent appearance, especially when compared to media models, they often need reassurance that their own worth is not solely dependent on how they look. Providing opportunities that allow young adolescents to identify other positive attributes of themselves is helpful.

Young adolescents' preoccupation with their appearance is evident by their frequent need to inspect their image in a mirror.

Another arena of development that impacts young adolescents psychologically is the timing of puberty. Most youngsters dislike being different from their peers; where an individual fits on the developmental continuum is obvious. While most adolescents would prefer to be average in terms of developmental timing, there are implications for those who physically mature early or later than others. Some gender differences that accompany the timing of puberty are discussed below.

According to Santrock (2005) it is advantageous for males to mature early. Since much of an adolescent male's social status and self-confidence are won through physical prowess usually displayed through athletics, it is an advantage to be bigger, stronger, and faster than one's peers. Interestingly, however, late-maturing boys are generally better adjusted and establish a more positive personal identity when they reach adulthood. On the negative side, since early-maturing boys tend to select older friends, they may be at a greater risk for early tobacco, alcohol, and drug use as well as other dangerous behaviors.

For girls, the impact of off-time development seemed to be both a blessing and a curse. Blyth and Simmons (1987) found that sixth-grade girls who developed early were more satisfied with their body image compared to their late-developing classmates. But by late adolescence the trend had reversed because many early-developing females tended to become endomorphic (i.e., short and stocky) while late-maturing females tend to develop the more ectomorphic (tall and lean) figure that is the more socially accepted body shape in our culture. Studies by Ge, Conger, and Elder (2001) indicate that early development for girls makes them more vulnerable to serious health problems and risky behaviors such as smoking, drinking, depression, eating disorders, earlier dating, and sexual experiences.

In working with young adolescents, it is important to keep in mind that early or late development alone is not likely a strong enough influence to predispose any individual to the problems or behaviors described above. Most people emerge from adolescence to become normal, healthy, and productive adults.

Young adolescents need to know about their development

The physical changes that accompany puberty inevitably produce some anxiety for young teens, but knowing what to expect as puberty unfolds is very reassuring. When a young girl discovers vaginal bleeding during her first period but is neither aware of the physiological significance of the event nor prepared to deal with the personal hygiene issues, what is she to think other than there is something terribly wrong with her body? When the developing male awakens with wet sheets following his first nocturnal emission, what is he to think other than this is not normal? Young adolescents need and deserve to know basic factual information about their own development as well as that of the opposite sex.

Parents generally are the best source of information since they know their own child and how he or she will respond to receiving sensitive information. I found that my son did not respond well to having "the talk." Finding examples and situations from everyday life to serve as a catalyst for discussing delicate issues worked much better for us. We frequently discussed episodes from network television programs, situation comedies, movies, or even the nightly news to broaden and confirm his knowledge of human development and sexuality. Such discussions also afforded my wife and me the opportunity to share our personal and family values with our son. Parents are the best source of personal information for their children, but public schools, even if they cannot delve into moral issues, play an important role in educating students about important developmental issues. When parents and responsible adults do not take this responsibility seriously, young teens will rely on the misinformation shared by peers and run the risk of adopting the irresponsible attitudes about sexual behavior shown in the media.

When parents and responsible adults do not take this responsibility seriously, young teens will rely on the misinformation shared by peers and run the risk of adopting the irresponsible attitudes about sexual behavior shown in the media.

Youngsters also need to know that the range and timing of normal human development is huge. I once asked a middle school student if he would like to be able to fly. His immediate response was yes, but then he quickly added, "But only if everyone else could." This exchange illustrates a young adolescent's fear of being viewed as "different" from his or her peers. Being different to a middle school student generally equates to being deficient or abnormal in some way. Late-maturing adolescents need to be assured that their developmental timetable is normal for them, while those on the fast track to physical maturation need to know that their friends will eventually catch up.

Implications for parents and teachers

Because young adolescents are going through vast physical changes, adults can help them adjust to this new life stage by being responsive and sensitive to those changes. Some suggestions for how adults can help young adolescents negotiate puberty follow:

- Early adolescence often is accompanied by an "awkward stage." Expect accidents and try to minimize their aftermath.
- Advanced physical development does not necessarily equate to intellectual or emotional maturity. Just because a teen looks like an adult does not mean that he or she is ready for adult responsibility.
- Expect the need for frequent movement. Due to abundant energy and hormonal fluctuations, young adolescents need to move frequently. Seldom are young adolescents still for any length of time.
- Allow and tolerate unusual postures. Since it is uncomfortable for young adolescents to sit on hard surfaces for extended periods, when given the chance they will shift positions often. Allow alternative seating positions. Students should view this as an accommodation and not abuse the privilege.
- Respect young adolescent modesty and need for privacy. The most obvious application of this principle in schools is in physical education classes. Most young adolescents, both male and female, resist gang showers and changing clothes in a common area. I remember students coming to my class from physical education who complied with the mandatory shower but did it by wearing their underwear. Some students wear their PE uniforms under their street clothes

to avoid changing clothes. There are many venues in which adults need to help provide adolescents with the privacy they desire.

- Avoid comparisons with peers and siblings. Young adolescents are trying to carve out their personal identity. Comparing them to others only confounds this effort.
- Recognize that physical appearance is linked to self perception. Youngsters should never be put in a situation that spotlights a physical deficiency. Parents should try, within reason, to help their children accentuate their physical attributes.
- Encourage youngsters to ask questions. But be sure to respond to the questions being asked.

A seventh-grade girl came home from school and asked her mother, "What's a diaphragm?" The mother seized the opportunity and informed her daughter about all sorts of birth control devices. The young girl listened carefully but was puzzled by her mother's explanation and responded, "Mom, I'm confused! My choral instructor today told us to sing from our diaphragm. What you just told me doesn't make any sense at all." The moral of the story is to make sure we answer the question being asked.

In summary

Early adolescence is an exciting but often confusing life stage. While many changes are taking place for the emerging adolescent, no other transformation is as obvious to the youngster as the physical changes that accompany puberty. Young adolescents will cope much better with the changes that they experience during puberty if they are well informed about the biological transformation that they will undergo as they mature. To know what to expect and to understand that what they are experiencing is a normal and natural process is reassuring. Young adolescents need and deserve parents, teachers, and other mature adults in their lives to provide accurate information about growing up and to reassure them that they are normal.

As some young adolescents see it …

The worst part of being a teen is all the pressure to be skinny.
Alexandra, age 14

I never used to wear makeup. I do now to cover up my flaws.
Jill, age 12

4.
Emotional Development

olatile vats of highly charged hormones ready to explode at any moment! Such an unflattering stereotype of young adolescents' emotional state exists. It is likely a remnant of the work of G. Stanley Hall (1884-1924) who published the first book on adolescence in 1904. Hall's pioneering work described the teen years as marked by extreme periods of emotional "storm and stress" and did much to advance serious consideration of adolescence as a distinct life stage and laid the foundation for more scientific study of this age group. But today, most experts believe that while adolescence is marked with emotional highs and lows, the teen years are no less stable than any other life stage. By characterizing early adolescence as a period of "storm and stress" it is too easy for adults to attribute real emotional problems of individual young teens to "raging hormones," or dismiss a serious episode as "just a phase" that will soon pass.

While the period of early adolescence frequently resembles an emotional roller coaster ride as moods change quickly, learning to deal and cope appropriately with a wide range of emotions is part of the maturation process. Yet, emotional maturity takes time and practice to develop. In this chapter I will describe the emotional traits of young adolescents and ways adults can respond appropriately to young teens' emotional needs.

Issues involving self

Young adolescents often exhibit behaviors that illustrate their self-centered natures. Playing music on their stereos at a volume that disturbs others in the household or even the neighborhood, monopolizing the family computer, or expecting parents to frequently rearrange their work schedule at a moment's notice to accommodate their own social agenda are examples of how young teens' behaviors or expectations tend to focus on their own personal desires. Such actions often seem selfish, rude, and inconsiderate to adults. Yet, young adolescents are surprised when adults "get on their case" about narcissistic behavior since they seldom realize how their actions are perceived by others. Many young adolescents are concrete, operational thinkers, having not developed the cognitive ability to put themselves in

55

the position of others. Therefore, they may have trouble interpreting their own actions from the perspective of people around them.

While rude and selfish behavior should not be tolerated or ignored, such episodes need to be dealt with delicately. Without judging, ask clarifying questions about how their behavior impacts others. Ask young teens to analyze what they would want others to do if a situation were reversed. My son and I recently were involved in an activity which required us to rise at 3:00 a.m. in order to participate in the event. I was trying to be extremely quiet to avoid disturbing the rest of the household as I prepared to leave. Yet, Casey was opening and closing dresser drawers and closet doors as he would on a school morning when everyone was up and awake. Casey values his sleep, so I calmly asked him to think about how he would want others to prepare for their day if they were up in the middle of the night and he was trying to sleep. He was not intentionally trying to be disruptive; it simply never occurred to him that he should make an extra effort to be quiet for the sake of others. All it took was a gentle prompt from me for Casey to muffle his movements about the house. Yet, it is not guaranteed that the lesson will carry over if the situation were to be replayed at a later date. It takes time for "others centered" behaviors and responses to develop and mature in young adolescents.

Adolescent egocentrism

When teaching about young adolescent development, I always emphasize adolescent egocentrism as the most pervasive trait of ten- to 15-year-olds. I base that claim on two decades of middle school teaching where I regularly observed countless examples of this behavior played out by scores of students. David Elkind (1976) defined this phenomenon as an increased sense of self-consciousness where individuals believe that others are as interested in them as they are in themselves. Elkind described the two components of adolescent egocentrism: the imaginary audience and the personal fable.

The *imaginary audience* is the belief that everyone's attention is centered on young adolescents when they are in the presence of others. For example, when a young adolescent girl has a bad hair day, she is convinced that all eyes focus on her unruly hair when she walks into a room. Similarly, a young adolescent boy is certain that everybody in the entire school had noticed when he discovered his unzipped fly. Young adolescents constantly feel that they are under the proverbial microscope and are "on stage" when in the presence of others. From the adult perspective it isn't that way, but for young adolescents, being in the spotlight for several hours a day is their reality. It is no wonder that many young adolescents come home from school, not only physically tired, but emotionally drained as well.

ISN'T IT ALL ABOUT ME?

Jerry is an excellent student and a key player on his middle school soccer team. On the afternoon of a big game, Jerry discovered that he had left his uniform socks at home. Knowing that his father was planning to attend the game, Jerry telephoned his father and asked him to swing by their home, pick up his socks, and deliver them to him prior to the start of the game. Jerry's father had already rearranged his tight work schedule so he could attend the match but Jerry's request now made it necessary for further alterations in his agenda. Jerry's dad raced home, managed to find the socks, and hurried to the field only to find his son in full uniform. When asked how he came up with the appropriate footwear, Jerry nonchalantly informed his dad that he borrowed them from a teammate who had an extra pair. Obviously, Jerry's father was exasperated. How should he respond?

1. Ground Jerry for a week for being irresponsible and inconsiderate.
2. Immediately explain to Jerry, sparing no detail, how the episode had disrupted his day.
3. Forget the episode, discounting it as just another example of adolescent immaturity.
4. Discuss the issue later in private, at home, and after his blood pressure had returned to normal.
5. Other _____

Comment:

This is a prime example of the self-centered nature of young adolescents. In Jerry's mind, picking up the forgotten socks was a very trivial matter, and he had no idea how disruptive it was to his father. Also, while calling his father was Jerry's first solution to his dilemma, it never occurred to him to call his father back to inform him that the problem was resolved. When the borrowed socks satisfied his needs, Jerry did not think about his father.

Such episodes as this make parents wonder if they are raising selfish and ungrateful kids. Option four above would be an appropriate strategy to deal with such a situation. Responding in anger would confuse Jerry since he might interpret the incident as his dad's making a big deal over a pair of socks. A calm and private discussion with Jerry about how the event impacted his father and how the situation could have been handled differently would be an appropriate response.

The *personal fable* involves an artificially elevated sense of uniqueness. This aspect of egocentrism causes young adolescents to believe that no one has ever experienced anything that is even remotely similar to the traumatic situations in which they frequently find themselves. For example, Megan is upset because her boyfriend of six weeks has just broken up with her. In her mind, she is the only person on the planet or in recorded history who has suffered such heartbreak. By the same token, Manuel is devastated because he was cut from the seventh-grade basketball team. In his adolescent way of thinking, he is a horrible basketball player and the only athlete in the world who has failed to make the team. When adults, or even peers, try to console such disappointment in young teens, they are frequently told, "You don't understand what I am going through!" or "Nobody understands me!" Such words often reveal that the personal fable is at work when no amount of logic or reasoning soothes the wounded spirit of a disheartened young adolescent. But just being willing to listen to a young teen's tale of woe is often the only and best thing to do.

An additional component of the personal fable has serious implications for the health and wellness of young adolescents. Along with an exalted sense of uniqueness comes a false sense of invulnerability. Many young adolescents believe they are "bulletproof"—nothing bad can happen to them. They hold the common belief that somehow being young shields them from negative consequences. Couple the invincible attitude with young adolescents' propensity for intense and risky behavior, and the potential for accidents and injury is extremely high. Young adolescents today have to make many choices that have long-term or even life-altering consequences, which previous generations did not. Young adolescents, for example, know about the addictive properties and health hazards associated with long-term tobacco use, not to mention marijuana, but the assumption that "bad things happen to other people, not me" negates the influence of that information.

As an advocate for this age group, I find the young teen attitude of immunity to misfortune both frightening and difficult to combat. When I taught middle school, I frequently clipped news reports of risky teen activities that ended tragically and shared them with my students at appropriate times. My students usually responded with blank stares and the sense that I was a dimwit for suggesting that this could happen to them. While it is not "cool" in teen culture to even suggest that adults might know what it is like being a teen today, parents and concerned adults need to cling to the hope that young adolescents will actually hear the counsel of adults in such matters and be led to make wise and responsible choices.

Independence versus security

Emotionally, young adolescents are very fragile. They vacillate between needing to establish adult independence while frequently requiring and still secretly desiring adult protection and security. Having a foot in both worlds of children and adults often creates situations that are confusing for young teens—and exasperating for adults.

Young adolescents vacillate between needing to establish adult independence while frequently requiring and still secretly desiring adult protection and security.

A bumper sticker advised, "Hire a teenager while she still knows it all!" This reflects a tendency of young teens to think they could solve complex problems. Inexperience, coupled with their idealistic ways of thinking, cause them to unravel complicated issues without thinking through or even being aware of all the contingencies involved. This "I've got it covered" attitude frequently comes across to adults as arrogance. Advice from adults is rejected since adults "don't have a clue!" While parents and teachers should, indeed, provide guidance for teens, there are times when young people need to apply their own solutions to problems, even when adults can see disaster looming on the horizon. It is hard for caring adults to watch a youngster "crash and burn." Obviously, adults need to intervene when a youthful solution to a problem is dangerous or has long-term ramifications; but adults should not be too quick to rescue young adolescents from wreckage of their own making. Experience is the best teacher. Maturity and wisdom are enhanced by having to live with the consequences of poor decisions. When young adolescents are dealing with the aftermath of failure, they need to be reassured that they are still loved and accepted. That refrain "I told you so!" should be avoided; just ask the young adolescent to think through what he would do differently to achieve a better result.

Identity formation

A major task of adolescents is to construct a personal identity—who they are as individuals, where they might go with their lives, and how they can fit into society. The works of Erikson (1968) and Marcia (1980) have traditionally been used to explain how personal identity is developed and achieved in our society. Their research focused mainly on personal, occupational, religious, and political aspects of identity formation in a Euro-American culture. More recent writers have emphasized the additional complexity of identity formation for U. S. youth who come from racially, ethnically, and culturally diverse backgrounds (Baldwin, Keating, & Bachman, 2006).

While Erikson's views on development spanned the entire human life cycle, two of his stages are of particular importance to middle level educators and parents. Children, according to Erikson (1968), work through the crisis of *industry versus inferiority*. They begin to form their views of self from the perspective of peers and other adults rather than from the perception of parents and family. Ten- and 11-year-olds tend to identify themselves by personal competency—activities and skills they perform well. Repeated success builds a sense of industry—that they are competent and valuable individuals. On the other hand, those students who struggle to find success in any endeavor create a sense of inferiority. The child who receives frequent and consistent messages that she is "no good" at art, math, or kickball, soon begins to believe that she is "no good" at all. Twelve- to 15-year-olds emerge into Erikson's fifth stage of development known as *identity versus identity* confusion, which lasts throughout adolescence. This stage of development is marked by exploration and experimentation as the young teen tries out numerous roles and experiences attempting to discover his true nature.

Marcia (1980) expanded on Erikson's work by suggesting four stages of identity formation experienced by most teens. Marcia believed the stages were dependent on the extent of exploration and level of personal commitment to an identity. The four stages Marcia described are

- Identity diffusion—a lack of exploration or commitment to any specific identity
- Identity foreclosure—the acceptance of an identity imposed by others without extensive exploration of other possible alternatives
- Identity moratorium—the exploration of many possible roles without any strong commitment to any of them
- Identity achievement—making a solid commitment to an identity after investigating and experimenting with many possibilities.

(pp. 159–187)

I have seen Marcia's stages of identity formation play out in the lives of many individual students. As a teacher, I worried about those students who had no goals. They were content to drift through life without exploring anything of value that life had to offer (identity diffusion). As a college professor in a rural state, I have known students who desired to pursue a profession but were expected to take over the family farm, a tradition that had existed for several generations (identity foreclosure). In my way of thinking, identity moratorium is an appropriate stage of identity development for middle level students. Investigating a wide variety of possible selves without putting them in conflict with other avenues of interest seems healthy for young adolescents (see case study following). One of the gratifying aspects of being a veteran educator is seeing former students achieve a positive occupational identity as adults. At some point in my teaching career, my auto mechanic, dental hygienist, barber, and physician's assistant were all former students. (I tried to remember if I ever gave these former students any reason to dislike me when they were entrusted with the care of personal property or used sharp instruments on my body!) Now as a teacher-educator, two of my past preservice teachers have served as my son's teachers.

Self-concept and self-esteem

Critics frequently malign middle level educators for paying too much attention to the affective needs of students—helping them feel good about themselves—at the expense of academic rigor. While the mission of any school should center on intellectual development, ignoring the affective domain, including promoting positive self-image, is counter productive. Middle school students simply learn best in an atmosphere where their social and emotional needs are addressed. How a student feels about herself is an extremely powerful emotional issue for teachers and parents to address.

Middle school students simply learn best in an atmosphere where their social and emotional needs are addressed.

Educators are prone to use terms such as self-esteem, self-concept, and self-image interchangeably when actually there are important differences in the meanings of each term. Page and Page (2003) used the image of a three-sided "social mirror" to explain how one constructs self-esteem. An individual standing in front of such a mirror, would see reflected back three perceptions of himself: (1) general perception, self-image; (2) how he would desire to be perceived, ideal self; and (3) awareness of how others view him, Pygmalion self. Self-esteem then is derived by evaluating all three components of self and constructing a global feeling known as self-esteem. If the total picture that evolves generally conveys the message that the individual is competent, valuable, and socially acceptable, then the individual emerges with a positive self-esteem. After examining the three dimensions of self, a negative self-esteem will be constructed if the individual sees himself as incompetent, all but worthless, and socially inept.

While self-esteem is a general evaluation of one's competency and worth, self-concept involves an assessment of one's competency in specific areas of endeavor. Harter (1989) developed the *Self-Perception Profile for Adolescents* as a useful tool for determining how adolescents form their self-concept. Harter determined that adolescents forge their self-concept around the following domains: scholastic competency, athletic competency, social acceptance, physical appearance, behavioral conduct, close friendships, romantic appeal, and job competence.

TOO MUCH TO EXPECT?

Jeff is an excellent athlete and enjoys several sports. His eighth-grade basketball coach stressed commitment to the sport and told the players that they needed to practice diligently year round. Making the team in high school would be contingent upon playing in several off-season leagues, attending basketball camps, and regularly participating in "open gym" during the summer months. At age 13, Jeff felt he was being asked to choose between basketball and others sports, as well as other activities he enjoyed. What should Jeff do?

1. Give up basketball.
2. Ask his parents to intervene with the coaches, asking them to ease up on expectations.
3. Petition the school board for more reasonable athletic policies.
4. Continue to be involved in other sports and activities and take his chances on making the high school team.
5. Other _____

Comment:

While teaching dedication and commitment to a goal is noble, it should not come at the expense of other components of development. Athletics are only one facet of Jeff's identity and dedication to one activity should not force him to abandon other interests. The middle level should be a time of exploration rather than specialization. In the classroom, concert stage, art studio, and athletic field, middle level students should be encouraged to explore many areas of interest rather than being forced to limit activities. One gifted middle level athlete broke off friendships with peers because he did not have time to spend with them. After practice and homework, there was no time or energy left for a social life—a heavy price to pay for a middle schooler.

The value that an individual places on each specific domain is a major factor in how that domain impacts one's overall self-concept. For example, Jenny works hard to make average grades but longs to be an honor roll student. Her inability to perform academically at the level she would like has a negative impact on her self-concept. Sally, on the other hand, excels academically but would rather be accepted by the social elite on her team. Since Sally does not really value her scholastic achievement, her success in an undervalued domain has little impact on building a positive self-concept. In other words, the domains one values highly have the greatest impact on one's self-concept.

Studies have found that young adolescents consistently cite physical appearance as the domain to which they ascribe the most value (Fox, Page, Peters, Armstrong, & Kirby, 1994; Harter, 1999). Following physical appearance, teens ranked social acceptance and athletic prowess as important contributors to their global self-esteem. Teens reported academic competence and behaving well to have the least impact on their self-esteem (Harter, 1993). It also should be noted that students who derive their self-worth from the level of approval they receive from their peers generally report lower levels of self-worth compared to classmates who construct their self-image based on more internal qualities (Harter, 1996).

Young adolescents consistently cite physical appearance as the domain to which they ascribe the most value.

I have used Harter's (1996) domains of development in conjunction with some generalizations and asked graduate students to reflect on their own self-concept construction as an adolescent. Those generalizations are

- Females tend to value more domains than males.
- Male self-concept is generated through personal achievement.
- Female self-concept is produced through social acceptance and the quality of interpersonal relationships they establish.

Informal polls conducted with students seem to verify the validity of these generalizations. Although Harter's eight domains of competence were established for adolescents, many of them apply to adults as well.

Importance of self-esteem

Self-esteem obviously plays a major role in the well-being of individuals and directly relates to their success, achievement, and overall mental health. Self-esteem is constructed around a sense of competency, confidence, and efficacy. Youngsters who have learned early in life that they can perform successfully in many arenas build confidence and a personal locus of control that carries over to many areas of their lives. They tend to view life's challenges more positively and see options they can pursue to reach personal goals and solve life's problems. This "can do" attitude is closely linked to what Bandura (2000) labels self-efficacy.

Beane and Lipka (1987) cited the following areas of endeavor to be closely associated with the self-esteem of young adolescents:

- Participation—Young adolescents who have developed self-confidence are more likely to respond in class and participate in extracurricular activities than those who suffer from low self-esteem.
- School completion—Students who have a history of school success have built a strong self-concept around academic competency. Such students tend to value school and see lifelong learning as a worth-

while enterprise. Their peers who have struggled academically likely view school as a drudgery to be endured until they are old enough to drop out.

■ Social status—Positive self-esteem is enhanced when a favored position and high status can be earned among one's peers. On the other hand, rejection or isolation by peers is a major factor in contributing to low self-esteem.

■ Behavior—Youngsters who feel good about themselves usually conduct themselves in ways that others find acceptable. Those with a negative self-image frequently behave in an abrasive manner, which puts them in conflict with others. (p. 6)

Beane and Lipka also observed that self-esteem seeks stability even if it is negative. "Persons with positive self-esteem tend to seek feedback from others which is favorable while those with negative self-esteem often act so as to receive negative feedback" (p. 7).

■ Self-direction—Students with high self-esteem are confident they can complete a task without constant supervision or the need for reassurance that they are on the right track.

■ Achievement—Students who have developed a strong sense of self-efficacy tend to do well in school. Conversely, students who believe they are not likely to succeed, regardless of how hard they try, don't do well in school. Years of being unsuccessful in school can lead to "learned helplessness" a condition that generally peaks during the middle school years and is difficult to remedy as a young adolescent matures. (p. 7)

More recently, several behaviors have been linked, along with other factors, to low-self esteem such as eating disorders, depression, victimization, and thoughts of suicide (Egan & Perry, 1998; Graham & Juvonen, 1998; McGee & Williams, 2000).

Middle school transition and self-esteem

For over a half century, the anxiety and stress brought on by the transition from elementary school to a larger middle level institution has been the focus of attention by many researchers. In many cases, moving to the middle level school has been reported to have a negative impact on the emotional well-being of young adolescents. Simmons and Rosenberg (1973) found that students moving to the middle level experienced a decline in self-image and an increased sense of self-consciousness. Moving from a smaller, more nurturing elementary school into a larger, more impersonal institution is often seen as the root of emotional discomfort for students in transition. A loss of status is associated with the transition to middle school. In one short summer, students in transition move from being the "big kids" in the building to the "little kids" on campus. When coupled with puberty and other disruptive factors such as family dysfunction, a loss of self-esteem for specific individuals is most likely. When the learning environment of the school is not in harmony with the developmental needs of its students, a decline in motivation and displays of negative behavior are sure to follow (Eccles & Midgley, 1989). Good middle schools, of course, conscious of the potential problems associated with making the transition to a new school, intentionally plan ways to build self-esteem, provide support, and establish a climate of caring where individuals are well known and actively involved.

Young adolescent girls and self-concept

It is also very common for girls to experience a drop in self-concept as they approach early adolescence (Baldwin & Hoffman, 2002). This loss of self-concept could be attributed to several factors. Physical appearance is a powerful force in molding the self-concept of adolescents, and young females are bombarded with countless media messages that portray an unrealistic standard of "feminine beauty." It is no wonder that many young girls see themselves as unattractive when compared to the latest bevy of supermodels. Girls tend to place value on more aspects that contribute to defining self than boys and thus are more vulnerable. In the realm of academic competency, girls are inclined to underestimate and downplay their own scholastic ability (Lundeberg, Fox, & Puncochar, 1994). According to Brown and Gilligan (1990) young adolescent girls are apt to buy into society's stereotypic ideas of how they should behave and what they should believe. Since there are these gender differences in how young adolescents forge their self-concept, caring adults need to provide ample opportunities for them to develop a positive self-image.

Improving self-esteem and self-concept

To think that we can "give" self-esteem to another person is simply incorrect. It cannot be injected, ingested, or absorbed via nice words. Self-esteem has to be constructed by each individual. And that construction of a positive sense of self comes through competency that is earned through achievement of a valued goal or mastering a respected skill. Some well-intended practices have been implemented in education to enhance or protect self-esteem. Liberal use of stickers and "smiley faces" on students' papers helps students feel good about themselves. Complimenting students on mediocre efforts to motivate them proves counterproductive. Some school boards have made administrative decisions to eliminate the recognition of valedictorians and salutatorians at high school graduation to guard against hurt feelings. Such practice may rob those who have distinguished themselves as scholars of a well-deserved honor.

I do believe that competition is healthy. We live in a competitive society and our economic system is based on competition. But middle level educators and parents need to guard against practices that can easily cross the line of healthy competition and become cutthroat rivalries which bring out the worst in human beings. The news media frequently publicize barbaric incidents where the push for excellence came at the expense of trampling on the dignity of others. The "do whatever it takes to get ahead" or "win at all costs" mentality, usually perpetuated by adults, almost always teaches powerfully inappropriate lessons to our youth. Striking the balance between encouraging excellence and appropriate recognition for achievement in any field of endeavor without separating young adolescents into "winners" and "losers" is the challenge for advocates of this age group.

Middle level educators and parents must do all they can to increase the probability that every student will be successful. Middle level advocate Conrad Toepfer advises teachers to "pitch it where they can hit it." In organized baseball for children the coaches want each child to be successful at the plate and will carefully lob every pitch into the strike zone so the batter will most likely make contact. If, after several pitches, hitting a moving target proves too difficult, the ball is placed on a tee.

Teachers need to offer multiple avenues to success by differentiating instruction, adopting high but realistic goals, altering pace, and using alternative forms of assessment and evaluation.

The baseball analogy is also true in the classroom. The objective is not to "strike out kids" but to enhance the possibility that every student will be able to get a base hit and even an occasional home run. To accomplish this, teachers need to offer multiple avenues to success by differentiating instruction, adopting high but realistic goals, altering pace, and using alternative forms of assessment and evaluation. Teachers can engineer learning situations that allow students to use their unique talents or abilities in ways that will help them earn status and recognition in the eyes of their peers. Students should set personal goals and measure their success in terms of self-improvement, rather than by besting others.

Here are practices and behaviors that teachers can employ that will help students achieve self-esteem:

- Get to know your students and call them by name.
- Help students recognize their personal talents and abilities.
- Help students set realistic goals.
- Encourage students to speak well of themselves and others.
- Support reasonable and safe risk taking.
- Encourage students to be active and involved in various activities.

- Listen carefully to young adolescents, especially to the words not spoken directly.
- Help students recognize that they will not always succeed.
- Focus on doing one's best rather than always striving for perfection.

Important formal lessons are learned in school, but possibly the most valuable and enduring lessons are those we learn about ourselves. This concept was captured by Wing (2001) who describes the challenge of planning meaningful learning experiences for her eighth-grade students by stating, "As they stretch their intellectual, physical, and creative boundaries, students need help balancing humility with a frank awareness of their strengths; balancing perseverance with an authentic look at their academic and personal weaknesses; balancing aspirations with limitations. Essentially, it's building confidence and competence simultaneously" (p. 40).

Emotional intelligence

Teachers, of course, hope that their students will grow into happy and successful adults. As educators, we frequently tell students that the road to success is paved with a good education. That advice implies that those who are more academically inclined and possess more intellectual ability have the inside track to success. In 1995, Daniel Goleman proposed that, while intellectual ability was an important factor in attaining success, other factors were even more critical. Goleman proposed that emotional intelligence, not traditional intelligence as measured by IQ tests, was more important in predicting and attaining adult success. Goleman maintained that managing one's emotions, empathizing with others, and handling personal relationships appropriately are essential skills to achieving success.

While educators quickly embraced the idea that there was more to being successful than being "book smart" others challenged Goleman's claims. Cobb and Mayer (2000) reported that the concept of emotional intelligence had to meet specific criteria before it could be recognized as a "psychological entity." One such criterion is that the ability must be measurable before it can be defined as an "intelligence." Two such measures of emotional intelligence have been devised—the *Mayer-Salovey-Caruso Emotional Intelligence Test* (MSCEIT) and the *Multifactor Emotional Intelligence Scale* (MEIS). Both tests attempt to measure four elements of emotional intelligence—perception, facilitation of thought, understanding, and management. While the jury is still out concerning the validity of the two intelligence tests, there is substantial evidence that emotional intelligence does exist as a discrete mental capacity (Mayer, Caruso, & Salovey, 1999).

Cobb and Mayer (2000) recognize that Goleman's claims of emotional intelligence as a strong predictor of adult success remain unsubstantiated, but they do report, rather conclusively, that those youngsters who score high on emotional intelligence tests avoid abrasive and aggressive behaviors and make wiser decisions about their personal health as adults.

While educators at all levels need to be cautious about turning emotional intelligence into an educational bandwagon, there is enough empirical evidence to support the idea that having command over one's emotions and the ability to establish positive relationships with others is important in living a successful life and in school success. News reports are filled with tragic stories where careers were ruined, political campaigns derailed, and lives destroyed when emotions ran unchecked. Business partnerships, friendships, and marriages frequently end when individuals fail to communicate and cooperate with each other. An emotionally intelligent individual knows when to speak—supported by the appropriate tone, facial expression, and body language—and when to remain silent.

Goleman (1995) outlined seven interpersonal and intrapersonal traits as being directly related to emotional intelligence and critical elements in how students learn:

- Confidence—A sense of control and mastery. One sees that she is more likely to succeed than fail.
- Curiosity—The sense that finding out about things is positive and pleasurable.
- Intentionality—The wish and capacity to have an impact and to act upon that wish with persistence.
- Self-control—The ability to modulate and control one's own actions in age-appropriate ways; a sense of inner control.
- Relatedness—The ability to engage with others based on the sense of being understood by and understanding others.
- Communication—The ability and desire to verbally exchange ideas, feelings, and concepts with others in an atmosphere of trust and respect.
- Cooperation—The ability to balance one's own needs with those of others. (p. 194)

Common sense tells us that students who develop the capacities outlined above, coupled with even average intelligence, will have a lot going for them in their personal quest for success and fulfillment. I don't think that it is necessary or desirable for schools to adopt formal programs or adapt the curriculum to foster emotional intelligence for their students. Teachers can use events that occur naturally in the course of their day to enhance emotional learning. Parents, likewise, aware of this concept, can use events in family life to do the same.

In today's climate of accountability with its increased scrutiny of schools based on standardized test scores, giving attention to emotional issues and concerns is likely to get short shrift. The narrow focus only on a small part of the academic domain is misguided when evidence shows that a positive emotional state leads to higher academic achievement (Franklin, 2005b). If we want to help students develop to their full potential, then no aspect of their development should be overlooked.

Emotional traits of young adolescents

Because young adolescents' emotions are so close to the surface, they are easily and readily revealed to anyone close by. Several emotional characteristics they frequently exhibit are discussed in the following paragraphs.

Moodiness. Young adolescents often display extremes of emotional highs and lows over a relatively short time span—elated one moment and then in despair an hour later. Moodiness has traditionally been attributed to normal hormonal fluctuations in adolescents, but parents and teachers should not be too quick to dismiss sullen behavior to puberty. While being responsive to a young adolescent's sensitivity, other aspects of a youngster's life should be examined.

Sense of crisis. When routine events occur that are not to the liking of adolescents, young teens often erupt in an emotional display that adults view as totally disproportionate to the event. Running out of their preferred breakfast cereal or not having their favorite jeans laundered on the day they wish to wear them may trigger a full-blown emotional outburst. To overreact seems to be a given right to young adolescents.

Fickleness. Early adolescence is a time for experimentation and exploration. It is normal for them to take up a new venture then quickly lose interest. While it is important for young teens to learn to follow through on their promises and commitments, the wise parent rents a clarinet, rather than buying it, when her daughter indicates she wants to join the band. Likewise, young adolescents frequently shift affiliations with friends and romantic interests as they move through the middle level years.

Devotion to causes. Because of the heightened sense of justice that seems to come to young adolescents, they are generally eager to take up humanitarian causes and work hard to convert others to their way of thinking. They may decide to become vegetarians in response to animal rights issues or oppose clear-cutting of forests in an effort to stem global warming. While the young teen's fervent support of noble causes is genuine, it is often short-lived and supplanted by another laudable endeavor.

Reaction to criticism. Young adolescents are easily offended. Even the most benign suggestion can be taken as a scathing personal attack. Most young adolescents detest being "yelled at" by adults. But adults and young teens define yelling differently. To adults yelling implies shouting, accompanied by a red face and bulging neck veins. But to a young adolescent, any negative comment from an adult, regardless of how tactfully couched, may constitute being "yelled at."

Impulsive. Young adolescents are novices when it comes to controlling impulses. They are prone to act upon their thoughts without thinking through the consequences of their actions. During an archery unit, two eighth grade boys conjectured how far an arrow might penetrate into the human body. One of the boys volunteered to be a human target while the other backed off several paces and proceeded to plunk his classmate with an arrow. Fortunately, the projectile struck the target's clavicle (collar bone), deflected into the shoulder muscle, and caused only superficial injuries. Obviously, if the arrow had struck a vital organ or major blood vessel, the results could have been tragic. Never once did the boys consider that their experiment could be life threatening.

Negative sense of self. When adolescents look at themselves in a mirror, they generally do not like the image. Few young adolescents are pleased with the way they look, and since appearance and body image are so closely tied to self-concept, it is no wonder that many young adolescents hold a negative view of themselves. I frequently ask graduate students to bring to class photographs of themselves when they were young adolescents. It is not unusual for adults to tell me that they could not find pictures of themselves at that age because they hated having their photograph taken and avoided it whenever possible.

Need for privacy. Because young adolescents are beginning to advance cognitively, they now can contemplate the future and speculate about options in their lives. Much occurs developmentally, and they require time to think things through. Thus young adolescents will spend what seems like hours in their rooms behind a closed door mulling over events and relationships. Also, most teens have a heightened sense of modesty due to their rapidly changing bodies. Their need for physical and emotional privacy should be respected.

Sense of humor. One thing middle level students fear most is being embarrassed or made fun of in front of their peers. Yet, young adolescent humor is often directed at others. Peers, adults, people with obvious differences are frequent targets of young teen humor. Poking fun at others is a way to deflect attention away from themselves so others will not notice perceived inadequacies. Sarcasm is a specific type of humor that young adolescents frequently inflict on each other. But sarcasm frequently results in hurt feelings since many teens interpret such humor literally. Exchanging good-natured verbal barbs is common among this age group. Status is earned by verbally out-dueling a classmate (Wormeli, 2003). Verbal put-downs are common among peers and even good friends. As long as all parties involved do not take such exchanges seriously or personally, then adults should not be concerned.

Stress. Stress is an inherent part of every life stage. But young adolescent stress seems to peak at a point when the individual has developed few coping skills to deal with adversity. Stress is exacerbated by the loss of control over one's environment, difficulties in finding status in peer relationships, and living in an unstable family. Anguishing over natural, social, and political issues is also a major cause of stress for young adolescents.

School is very definitely a source of stress for young adolescents. Academic demands can place a psychological squeeze on students, especially major exams or oral reports. Developmentally responsive middle level teams provide practice sessions for oral reports and coordinate their assignments so students don't face an unreasonable amount of homework on a given day. Parents should be involved in establishing homework guidelines and policies.

Dealing with the emotions of young adolescents

Keep things in perspective. While teachers and parents as significant adults in the lives of young teens may bear the brunt of emotional outbursts, they should try not to take such eruptions personally. The flare-up is likely related to some other issue or person. But the youngster feels comfortable venting in your presence because he knows you will hear him out and still love and care for him regardless of his volatile behavior.

Listen. Above all else, young adolescents want adults who will listen carefully to their concerns and complaints. Offer advice if it is solicited, but just the opportunity to talk things through is often enough to help middle level students arrive at an appropriate solution or response.

Take concerns seriously. Sometimes it is difficult to keep a straight face when young adolescents come to you with an earth-shattering problem that seems frivolous from an adult perspective. Know that every social gaffe and shun from a peer can be a cause for emotional trauma for a young teen. Empathizing with their problems, rather than trivializing them, is the kind of emotional first-aid needed by wounded young adolescents.

Dear Diary,

I can't believe I go from feeling great to feeling terrible. What's worse is that I seem to go from wonderful highs to horrible lows. This is a typical roller coaster ride for me each day. Unfortunately, it's usualy downhill!

— from *Love Me When I'm Most Unlovable* by Robert Ricken

71

IS THIS A GOOD IDEA?

Mr. O'Hare, the English teacher on his seventh-grade team, is an ardent environmentalist. The state standards dictate that he teach persuasive writing skills to all students. As a final assessment for this unit on the genre, Mr. O'Hare required his students to compose and send a letter to one of their legislators asking him to oppose oil and gas exploration in national wildlife sanctuaries. Is this an appropriate assignment?

1. This is a good example of using authentic assessment since the letters will be read by a real audience and deal with a genuine issue.
2. Students will be motivated to complete the assignment since it deals with an issue they have been studying.
3. Dictating the subject and stance of the letter forces students to advocate for something they may not believe in.
4. Other _____

Comment:

As a passionate environmentalist, Mr. O'Hare is strongly opposed to the government's sanctioning the extraction of oil and gas from areas set aside to protect wildlife. Engaging students in real issues is a powerful and effective instructional strategy. But promoting a point of view students should take on such an issue is unethical behavior on the part of the teacher. Adults need to guard against exploiting young adolescents' propensity for getting involved in causes in order to advance their own personal agendas.

Be a good role model. While it is not possible to teach or project positive self-esteem or emotional stability on students, one can be a model of what a self-confident and well-adjusted adult looks and acts like. This means that adults must take care of themselves physically and emotionally to remain a positive presence in the lives of youngsters.

Provide legitimate praise and appropriate reinforcement. Clerks at most retail stores are trained to thank customers for shopping and to say "have a nice day." Patrons can detect if the clerk is sincere or not. So it is with young adolescents. What is being praised, indeed, should be praise-worthy and your words offered sincerely. Acclaim should be specific, focusing on some aspect of a project that was done especially well. Since being singled out in front of the entire class even for doing a good job might put a student at odds with her peer group, such recognition may be given in a more subtle or private way.

Understand and accept normal behavior. When Casey was a small child he threw a tantrum in a grocery story. In frustration, I knelt down to make direct eye contact and reprimanded him by saying that he was acting like a four-year-old! I had no more gotten the words out of my mouth when I realized that he was four years old. Why was I surprised that he was behaving in an age-appropriate manner? The same applies to young adolescents. Their immature and irresponsible actions are often frustrating to adults close to them but are quite normal. Young adolescents provide the raw materials from which responsible adults are made—but they have to be molded.

Remember what it was like. Young adolescents do not generally respond well to conversations that begin, "When I was your age …" But it is good for adults to relive, in their own minds, some of their own triumphs and tragedies of young adolescence. Such reflections often provide needed perspective on conditions that seem trivial to them now.

In summary

The developmental domains of young adolescents are intertwined and impact each other. But the emotional domain is the vent through which the internal pressure of growing up escapes. Young adolescents are extremely focused on self and are concerned about how others perceive them. At no other life stage are they more apprehensive about how they measure up compared to others, especially their peers. Also, during early adolescence, young teens detect more developmental differences between themselves and others. This perceived dissonance between themselves and others is generally interpreted as a personal deficiency, which results in a negative view of self. The frustration and inadequacy young adolescents feel on numerous fronts results in emotional magma that boils to the surface. Nearly all young teens will eventually develop effective coping skills and a more mature perspective of self. In the meantime, they need and deserve caring adults in their lives who will give them the space they require to grow, but who are also close by to provide emotional support and first aid when needed.

As some young adolescents see it …

They say that being an adult is tough.
But what is tougher is getting there.
Jimmy, age 14

It hurts when adults do not take my opinions seriously
as they would if I was an adult.
Lilly, age 14

At our age, we are really developing personalities. And although we may not be what you expect, we can only be ourselves.
Amelia, age 12

Does it get any better as you get older?
Emily, age 14

I wish I could express my feelings so adults would understand what I am going through.
Carley, age 13

One day I am happy and the next day I am sad. Is this a normal part of growing up?
Laura, age 12

5.

Moral, Religious, and Character Development

The ability of individuals to consider the needs, rights, and wants of others when deciding upon personal behaviors is a major staple of a civilized society. When just staying alive and eking out an existence dominated the time and energy of prehistoric people, probably little thought was given to whether acting on their survival instincts was moral or ethical. Even in modern times, normally civil humans resort to barbaric behaviors when their personal survival is threatened. News reports from the scenes of natural disasters often depict discrepant examples of the best and worst of human behavior. When the gulf coast of the U. S. was ravaged by a devastating hurricane, legions of people put their own lives in jeopardy to assist those in peril. At the same time, unfortunately, others looted and plundered businesses and homes of fellow citizens. Civilized societies depend on people consistently behaving in ways that promote the common good and welfare of all people. So how does an individual learn to behave in a moral and ethical manner? Who is responsible for helping young people develop a noble character?

From the outset, we need to affirm the fact that families, especially parents, are a child's first and most effective teacher in all areas of development; but middle level schools play a particularly critical role in shaping the moral and ethical nature of young people.

The role of formal education

How individuals develop a sense of right and wrong and how they apply those standards to govern their thoughts and interactions with others is the essence of moral development. For centuries, teachers and philosophers have included moral development as an essential element of an educated person. In the fourth century B.C., both Plato and Aristotle spoke about the importance of promoting the moral nature of youth by enhancing their intellectual abilities and responding to ethical issues (Vincent, 1999).

Many religions have established schools to ensure that a desired spiritual perspective would be inherent in the curriculum. Public schools in the United States have long been viewed as agents for perpetuating basic virtues and values—patriotism, loyalty, and good character, for example. Teachers were expected to be models of virtue, and employment was contingent upon maintaining a spotless reputation and demonstrating public conduct that was above reproach. Teachers today are still held to high standards of personal behavior both in and out of the classroom. Classrooms are still seen as places where values such as punctuality, respect, fairness, responsibility, neatness, and hard work have been honored and encouraged. Schools have always issued deportment or conduct grades as recognition that character development was an important part of an education.

As long as our society was fairly homogeneous, the question of what virtues to promote in public schools was rarely a problem. As a grade school student raised in a predominately Caucasian, Protestant, conservative small town in the Midwest, I remember starting each school day with the teacher leading us in the *Pledge of Allegiance* and reciting the *Lord's Prayer* without issue or objection. School-sponsored Christmas pageants were common and expected. But as our nation became more diverse, the role of schools in promoting cultural norms and virtues came into question. As our nation became more heterogeneous, coupled with the misguided perception that a solid academic curriculum was all people needed to succeed in an industrial economy, the moral development of students became less intentional in schools. In the name of "political correctness," and to avoid confrontation and even lawsuits, many teachers shied away from discussing moral and ethical issues with their students. Some opponents of morality being addressed at school claimed that such issues should be the domain of the family and church and that schools should attend only to the intellectual development of students—as if they could be neatly separated.

Current status of moral development and character education

Educators recognize that cognitive learning does not occur in a vacuum and that students cannot leave social issues at the school's door. In the early 1960s, teachers reported talking in class, failure to complete homework, and dress code violations as major problems. Today, teachers frequently deal with more serious concerns such as teen violence, substance abuse, and overt acts of disobedience. As I wrote this chapter, news reports told of a 15-year-old who shot down his assistant principal and wounded other school administrators. Such acts were unheard of 50 years ago. While the major role of school continues to be advancing the intellectual ability of students, most schools, especially middle schools, still recognize the importance of positive character development as a part of their mission. As one of the five stated goals for young adolescents, the authors of *Turning Points* (Carnegie Council, 1989) enumerated "a caring and ethical individual" as an outcome (p. 15). Dudley Flood, during his keynote address at the 2001 New England League of Middle Schools Conference listed the need for middle schools to help young adolescents develop a "spiritual proficiency"—a sense of appropriateness they can use to judge the difference between right and wrong—as a proper function of middle schools. Almost all middle level teachers and parents regard character development as an important part of their role as a significant adult in the lives of young adolescents, but it may get less direct attention than formerly.

Character education is defined as "the deliberate effort to cultivate *virtue*" (Lickona, 1999, p. 23). I emphasize the term virtue here since the word "values" is often used interchangeably when the affective domain is discussed. The word *value* carries with it the connotation of ascribed worth and personal preference. Values can be extremely positive or terribly destructive. Civic organizations, for example, claim to promote patriotism. On the other hand, groups who promote racial supremacy also claim to highly value patriotism but support it through bigotry and hate. The term *virtue* is associated with an attribute that has a positive and uplifting impact on an individual and those around him. The controversy that clouds the issue of schools promoting moral development or character education is the set of standards that are used to judge the degree of appropriateness when considering dilemmas or guiding one's behavior.

To avoid accusations of encouraging values that promote specific political, moral, or religious agendas, schools try to support behaviors and attitudes that are universally accepted as noble, constructive, and useful to help students attain school success. Attributes such as respect, responsibility, self-discipline, cooperation, tolerance, persistence, and honesty are examples. Few rational adults would object to institutions fostering such qualities in their clientele.

Theories of moral development

Jean Piaget. As is true with Piaget's theory of cognitive development, how a person thinks in moral terms becomes more sophisticated as one matures. Piaget was a keen observer of human behavior and formed much of his theory of human moral development by watching children at play and asking them questions. His study of children led Piaget to conclude that they go through two stages of moral development:

Heteronomous morality—Between the ages of four and seven, children believe that rules govern behavior and the resulting consequences of keeping or breaking rules is a universal and nonnegotiable fact of life. Strict adherence to rules set by a higher authority constitutes moral behavior at this stage. For a child at the heteronomous stage of moral development, considering the consequences of the behavior, rather than the intentions of the actor, is of primary importance when judging the correctness of a specific action. In other words, a child at this stage of moral development is most concerned about being punished if caught behaving poorly (Vincent, 1999). Piaget also proposed that heteronomous children believe in *imminent justice*—the notion that if a rule is broken, the wrongdoer will be punished immediately. By the same token, if a young child at this stage of moral development observes something unfortunate happen to a peer, he often concludes that the injured party did something wrong to bring on the calamity.

Autonomous morality—Children age 10 and older have learned that rules are created by people, are fluid, and can be negotiated. Piaget believed that peer relationships, where children learn to cooperate and solve disputes through compromise, were important aspects of moral development for children. For the autonomous child, the motivation behind one's action, rather than simply the outcome of the action, is of considerable importance when judging the morality of behavior.

Piaget's theory of moral development exhibits close similarities to his theories about how youngsters mature cognitively. As youngsters reach adolescence and become more abstract in their thinking, they are no longer tied to the "here and now" thinking that dominated their childhood and heteronomous morality. As young adolescents mature, they are more capable of "seeing the big picture," understanding situations from multiple perspectives, and separating the real from the ideal world, all cognitive functions essential to develop higher levels of moral reasoning (Santrock, 2005).

Cognitive disequilibrium theory. Building upon Piaget's ideas of moral development, Hoffman (1980) presented the theory that adolescents begin to adapt and adjust their thinking as they become exposed to more diverse ways to consider moral and ethical issues. The moral viewpoints of children are often closely linked to those of parents and other family members. As the circle of friends increases, a child is exposed to different ways of thinking about morality. As adolescents, youngsters are frequently presented with situations that are in conflict with the moral stance they have accepted as truth from childhood. They begin to consider, perhaps for the first time, that more than one viewpoint exists. The youngster is then left to decide if what constitutes right from wrong is at one end of the spectrum or the other, or somewhere in between. Hoffman suggested that adolescents are most likely to experience such disequilibrium when they move from a relatively homogeneous environment to a more heterogeneous setting, such as the transition from elementary school to middle school

Lawrence Kohlberg. One of the most well-known theories of moral development was proposed by the late Lawrence Kohlberg. The Harvard University scholar extended Piaget's thoughts concerning moral reasoning of children by studying adolescents. By interviewing teenage boys and asking them to respond to moral dilemmas, Kohlberg theorized that there are three distinct levels of moral development and each level is composed of two separate stages.

Kohlberg called the basic stage of moral reasoning the precon-ventional level. At this juncture, individuals are motivated by avoiding punishment and achieving personal gratification. People at this level of moral development are very self-centered and are guided by personal gain or loss. As individuals mature, most advance to Kohlberg's second level of development, the conventional level. Individuals at the conventional level seek to please others and maintain positive relationships. Avoiding conflict is important to the conventional thinker. They tend to conform to what is expected of them and try to be fair in their dealings with others.

Kohlberg's highest level of moral development was described as the postconventional level. At this stage a person's moral thinking is dominated by ideals of universal justice. Such an individual works hard at maintaining social order so long as it is not in conflict with what is best for the common good of others. Kohlberg believed that most children, delinquent teens, and adult criminals were at the preconventional level of moral development. He estimated that the majority of adults were at the conventional level while only about 20 percent of adults ever progressed to the postconventional stage. Kohlberg found that individuals needed to progress from one stage to another, that skipping a stage was not possible. He also found that an individual's moral thinking is fairly predictable in that people are prone to behave in ways that are consistent with their level of moral reasoning. At the lower levels of moral thinking people tend to be motivated to avoid punishment meted out by others. "Getting caught" is a major concern. At higher levels of morality, individuals are more concerned about living with a "guilty conscience" and avoiding self-condemnation. Kohlberg also suggested three possible ways that individuals evolve from one stage of moral development to another. One possible path involves a child's internalizing the set of beliefs and ideals modeled by the adults around her. Other factors proposed by Kohlberg that could advance a person's moral thinking are intellect, self-esteem, and ability to delay gratification. Finally, Kohlberg believed that humans possess the innate ability to detect when individuals are being treated fairly, a concept he called the *principle of justice* (Dacey & Kenny, 1997).

Carol Gilligan. While Kohlberg's theory did much to advance the thinking about how humans develop morally, Gilligan (1982) pointed out that Kohlberg's theory was biased against women since his subjects were exclusively male adolescents. After conducting extensive research, based on interviews with adolescent girls and young women contemplating serious moral decisions, Gilligan concluded that males and females approach moral decisions from different perspectives. In her view, males tend to view moral issues from justice orientation while women tend

Gilligan concluded that males and females approach moral decisions from different perspectives.

to focus more on interpersonal care as their moral center of gravity. Rice (1996) summarized Gilligan's views on gender differences in moral development by saying: "Men emphasize justice—preserving rights, rules, and principles. Women emphasize concern and care for others and sensitivity to their feelings and rights. Women emphasize responsibility to human beings rather than to abstract principles" (p. 315).

Even today, when many gender barriers have been removed in occupations, the fact remains that most nurturing and care-giving roles and occupations are filled by women. This fact is empirical evidence that Gilligan's views on moral development of females are on target. Her philosophy was not intended to supplant Kohlberg's theory of moral development but to supplement it. She argued that Kohlberg's theory did not adequately reflect the female orientation toward moral development; and being grounded in interpersonal care, it was as noble as the rights and justice inclination of males (Rice, 1996).

Moral development and young adolescents

Young adolescents are at a pivotal stage of life. Many of the beliefs, attitudes, values, and virtues they develop as young teens will go with them into their adult lives. As both Piaget and Kohlberg suggested, the ability to make solid moral and ethical decisions improve as their cognitive abilities become more sophisticated. Also, the phenomenon of "blooming and pruning" neurological pathways in the brain, referred to in Chapter 1, come into play when moral development is considered. According to the blooming and pruning theory, the nerve pathways that are used frequently become hardwired while those that are seldom activated are pruned away as dead wood. So if a youngster's mind is saturated with conventional morality as portrayed by the media and music so prevalent in today's pop culture, those messages begin to color young adolescents' views of right and wrong or good and bad. In response to neurological hardwiring of young adolescents' brains and to balance the impact of living in today's culture, Rick Wormeli (2003) wrote, "We middle school teachers need to provide even more experiences involving moral and abstract reasoning, planning, awareness of consequences, and the effects of one's words and actions on others, not fewer" (p. 10). With this idea in mind, let's explore how middle level educators can make positive impacts on the healthy moral development of young adolescents.

Moral development and character education—A middle level response

In today's climate of intense academic accountability, many educators feel that time devoted to anything but the academics is something they can't afford. But true middle schools have always addressed the affective, as well as the academic, needs of young adolescents. In fact, the entire September 2002 issue of *Middle School Journal* was devoted to the theme, "Nurturing Good People." Recently there has been an increase in the number of books and articles published about character education and moral development. Several states have incorporated the promotion of civic and social responsibility as a part of state standards. The challenge is to promote "good character" in a "politically correct" fashion without indoctrinating students in what to believe concerning moral and ethical issues. But fully functioning middle schools have a built-in organizational feature that is a perfect stage for young adolescents to explore the moral and ethical dimensions of being human and behaving humanely—a teacher advisory program.

Teacher Advisory (TA) programs have been a staple of good middle level schools for decades. Over the years advisory programs have been used to encourage teamwork, build community, foster a sense of belonging, and provide a forum for discussions on non-academic matters. Some middle schools use the TA concept specifically for character education. For example, Deitte (2002) reported incorporating active learning with character education as a focal point for a successful advisory program for sixth-grade middle schoolers. Using cooperative activities and role playing, followed by oral reflection, Deitte successfully nurtured these 10 universally accepted character traits: *respect, perseverance, integrity, citizenship, trustworthiness, responsibility, compassion, honesty, self-discipline,* and *fairness.* What rational adult would find fault in promoting such positive core values among our young people?

Turning Points (Carnegie Council on Adolescent Development, 1989), charged middle level schools to help students be "caring and ethical individuals" (p. 15). Formal courses cannot teach compassion and fairness to young people; such attitudes and dispositions must be developed over time from modeling and firsthand experiences. Service learning is one vehicle through which young adolescents

Service learning is one vehicle through which young adolescents can find connections between civic engagement and their academic studies.

can find connections between civic engagement and their academic studies. News reports frequently report on schools' being involved in relief efforts. While such initiatives are commendable and raise awareness of young students about the plight of others, such projects would not technically qualify as service learning. Allen (2003) cited three criteria from a report from the National Commission on Service Learning that make a service learning project worthwhile and distinguishes service learning from simply volunteer work. A true service learning project should include clear connections to academic content, satisfy a real need in the community, and involve students directly in planning, implementing, and assessing the success of the project.

There is much about the nature of service learning that supports the tenets of middle school philosophy. Successful service learning projects are student driven, constructivist in nature, personally meaningful, and actively engaging. When service learning is linked to national or local academic standards, the project adds true relevance to academic learning (Allen, 2003; Kielsmeier, 2000). While hard research data to support service learning are limited, Billig (2000) listed many reports that touted the merits of service learning. Her summary stated, "middle school students who engaged in high quality service learning programs showed increases in measures of personal and social responsibility." She went on to say that youngsters who were active in service learning projects were concerned with treating peers kindly, more prone to be helpful to others, and took pride in doing their best work. Teacher Advisory programs are often the platform to support service learning projects as a way to encourage caring and ethical behavior and attitudes among young adolescents.

Components of character education programs

A banner hangs in the lobby of an elementary school I frequently visit that proclaims

Character is what you do when nobody is watching!

This banner encompasses three components of character education which include *moral knowing, moral thinking,* and *moral acting* (Lickona, 1991). According to Lickona, schools that desire to intentionally impact the moral and character development of their constituents need to implement these six steps:

- Publicly identify specific core values that the school supports and embraces.
- Define the core values in terms of observable behavior.

- Model the core values consistently.
- Recognize and celebrate when behavior is consistent with the core values.
- Teach the application of the core values in all parts of school life and environment.
- Expect all school members, students and adults, to exhibit behavior that is consistent with the school's core values. (p. 37-45)

Character education programs can help provide students with multiple opportunities to develop the internal motivation needed to consistently behave in a responsible and respectful manner. Obviously, parents and family should be the major front where morals and character are shaped with the school playing a major supporting role. In many cases, young adolescents are navigating through life with a moral rudder that is either broken or missing. In those cases, the school and other community and civic organizations have to provide principled guidance for students.

Schools inevitably play a major role in molding the character of their students. But I believe that programs come with the warning, "batteries not included." Caring and competent people are needed to implement programs and provide the spark to make them effective. Youngsters take cues to guide their behavior by watching the adults close to them. "The moral development of students does not depend primarily on explicit character education efforts but on the maturity and ethical capacities of the adults with whom they interact" (Weissbourd, 2003, p. 1). In addition to being positive role models for students, the teachers' role goes far beyond helping students develop moral and ethical attributes. Weissbourd went on to say:

The best thing about being 14 is discovering all the possibilities I have for my future and the skills I didn't know I had. It seems anything is possible for the future. — An eighth grader

> Educators influence students' moral development ... by what they bring to their relationships with students day to day: their ability to appreciate students' perspectives and to disentangle them from their own, their ability to admit and learn from moral error, their moral energy and idealism, their generosity, and their ability to help students develop moral thinking without shying away from their own moral authority. That level of influence makes being an adult in a school a profound moral challenge. (p. 1)

A Lesson Learned?

Jim, a rookie middle level teacher and avid sports fan, was delighted when he was asked to coach the seventh-grade basketball team. At the beginning of the season, Jim announced to his team that every player would be a "starter" in at least one game during the season. As the season progressed, Jim made sure that he placed different players into starting positions each game. During the final game of the season, Jim was certain that he had fulfilled his promise to his team and started his best five players. After the game, Justin sat dejected in the corner of the locker room following a victory in the season finale. Sensing that something was terribly wrong, the coach sat down next to Justin and asked if there was a problem. Justin looked up at the young coach and seethed, "You lied to me!"

Somehow the season had passed and Justin was never in the starting lineup. Remembering his coach's promise and knowing that this was the final game of the season, Justin was positive that tonight he would be honored as a starter. Several of Justin's family members attended the game to share his moment in the spotlight—but it didn't happen. What should the coach do now?

1. Tell Justin that he is sorry and let it go at that.
2. Let it go since the season is over and nothing can be done about the situation.
3. Ask Justin what he as the coach can do to make amends for his mistake.
4. Talk privately with Justin, assure him that the mistake was not intentional, and admit to Justin he was wrong and terribly sorry for the error.
5. Make an excuse for why Justin did not start the game.
6. Other _____

Comment:

Young adolescents expect adults to uphold their promises. When we do not follow through on our word, our credibility with young adolescents is eroded. How we respond when we disappoint young adolescents sends powerful messages about our character.

I was this coach and was deeply saddened that I had disappointed this young athlete. I had violated his trust and put him in an awkward position with his family. I spoke privately with Justin after he dressed and apologized for my mistake. I also apologized to his family. That evening I wrote Justin a note to assure him that the slight was unintentional. While there was no way to really make amends, I wanted Justin to know that I was truly sorry.

ADDENDUM TO THE CASE STUDY: Twenty years later, I attended an annual festival in my small hometown in southern Indiana. A young man walked up to me and introduced himself as Justin. After exchanging the usual pleasantries, Justin asked me if I remembered the final game of our seventh-grade basketball season. Justin was not referring to the fact that we had won the game. I assured him that I remembered vividly the details of the evening. Justin told me he appreciated the note I sent him and that he still had it in his possession. I was glad to know that I had apparently handled a bad situation in a satisfactory manner and that Justin had not been scarred for life. I was reminded about the significance of this event in his life, an important lesson for both of us.

Walking the talk

Students quickly notice if the adults around them conduct themselves in ways consistent with the espoused moral code of the school. One school was embroiled in a contentious teachers' strike that divided the faculty and the entire community. Even after the strike was settled the various factions in the school were not on speaking terms and avoided contact with each other. Observing the behavior of adults around them, students learned that a Vermont State Standard 3.11 which they were expected to embrace, "Students interact respectfully with others, including those with whom they have differences," (Vermont Department of Education, 2000) was not being modeled by their teachers. In his classic work, *A Place Called School,* John Goodlad (1984) found that there is often a huge discrepancy between what schools claim to be their core values and what plays out in the culture of the school. When students experience that vast gulf between what they experience and what is touted as virtuous, students become skeptical and view the school's attempt to mold positive character traits as a charade. It is so important that students see and experience those adults close to them as individuals whose lives are examples of decency, integrity, and fair play.

Young adolescents and religion

Middle level education is founded on meeting the developmental needs of young adolescents and supporting the education of the whole child. Yet, many middle level educators avoid delving into the spiritual domain with students even though this segment of their lives is primed for investigation and exploration. Because young adolescents are beginning their identity search, religious faith and beliefs can help them figure out who they are and what they stand for as an individual. Since young adolescents are more abstract in their thinking, they may question the religious beliefs they were taught as a child and begin to explore the doctrines of other denominations or faiths. They are more prone to introspection and reflect on all aspects of their lives, including spirituality. The search for meaning and sense of belonging, both important issues for young adolescents, can often be met through participation in religious organizations.

Religious faith is a matter regularly on the minds of adolescents. Gallup and Bezilla (1992) found that the majority of teens they surveyed said they believed in God or a higher moral authority, prayed to a superior power, and felt it was important to identify with a religious faith. Religious convictions can play an important role in helping young teens make wise choices in the many health and wellness issues they confront. While the spiritual dimension is an important facet of an adolescent's total development, it is largely skirted by the public school system.

Clearly, public schools cannot promote a specific religious perspective or indoctrinate youngsters with a particular spiritual dogma. Concerns about First Amendment rights and the separation of church and state often cause educators to avoid religious or spiritual concepts in the normal classroom discourse. Recently, a school board in Florida ruled to eliminate ALL religious holidays from their calendar, such as Good Friday, Easter Monday, and Yom Kippur, when members of a particular faith requested to have an additional religious observance acknowledged by their schools. Such a knee-jerk reaction denies, in effect, the existence and importance of the spiritual realm of students and perpetuates intolerance among people from diverse religious backgrounds. Instead of avoiding religion, Lickona (1999) suggested seven strategies that public schools can embrace to incorporate religious concepts as part of a culture's fabric and encourage character education while avoiding controversy and conflict.

1. Schools can help students understand the role religion has played in our moral beginnings as a nation.
2. Schools can teach that our country's major social reform movements … have been inspired by a religious vision.
3. We can help students understand the role of religious motivation in the lives of individuals, both in history and in current times.
4. Schools can select or construct specific curricula so as to include religion.
5. Schools can encourage students to make use of all their intellectual and cultural resources, including their faith traditions, when they consider social issues and make personal moral decisions.
6. Schools can draw upon religion as a way to engage students in considering the question, Is there moral truth?

7. Schools can challenge students to develop a vision of life that addresses ultimate questions. (pp. 22–26)

There are ways that teachers can enhance students' spiritual literacy and character education without trampling on the constitutional rights of young people, but it is a difficult task at best. Religious and nonreligious students alike should be enlightened by investigating what various spiritual traditions have to say about social and moral issues that face our society. To include the religious lens as one of many to examine historical events is an excellent strategy that would add vigor and richness to the curriculum. The teachings of virtually all religions promote similar beliefs concerning how people should conduct themselves and treat others. Examining the major tenets of various religions or of those professed by individual students is a valid way to counter the nonchalant attitude the media portray about many moral and ethical issues in our society. While public school teachers need to be careful about promoting any specific religious philosophy over another, the spiritual domain should not be ignored. To do so flies in the face of the commitment to educate the whole child.

In summary

While there are those who say the public schools should attend only to the academic needs of students, most educators and parents recognize and support the position that an important role of the public school is to foster affective traits as well. The affairs of the heart are as important as those of the head. Young adolescents are at a point in their lives when they are developing attitudes, values, and beliefs that will remain with them for a lifetime. As it should be, parents play the largest role in shaping the character and morals of their children; but teachers are a major force in helping students develop a sense of propriety and justice. While many schools have implemented programs to enhance moral development and character education, good character cannot be developed by completing a set of exercises. Good character must be modeled by the significant others in students' lives. Young adolescents need to be surrounded by adults who consistently respond with integrity to negative situations, who will admit when they have made mistakes, and will do whatever is within their power to correct them.

Young adolescents are primed for moral development, and the schools they attend must help develop positive values, virtues, and character. By providing teacher advisory programs, service learning experiences, and investigating religious aspects and ethical issues through interdisciplinary studies, the moral development and character education of young adolescents will be furthered.

As some young adolescents see it …

Loyalty is an important part of being a friend.
Sasha, age 13

Parents and teachers should let us learn from our mistakes.
Johanna, age 13

*We don't need to be told what to do all the time
but sometimes we do.*
Kassie, age 12

*I stand up to adults more than I used to because they are not as tall
and scary looking now.*
Thomas, age 14

*We are not perfect and are going to mess up. So cut us a little slack
once in a while.*
Zack, age 13

I want somebody to help me reach my goals in life.
Jeff, age 14

CONTEXTS IN WHICH YOUNG ADOLESCENTS FUNCTION

Young adolescents are persons before, when, and after they assume the role of students engaged in formal education. And whole persons do, indeed, come to school bringing with them considerable baggage from their out-of-school lives—a reality teachers recognize and seek to accommodate every day. In a comparable way, the education of young adolescents does not come to a halt when school is out; for they, by nature, are explorers actively seeking meaning in events and conditions they experience. As they observe, listen, and interact with various situations in the environment, their education is ongoing.

Two major out-of-school contexts are especially important in shaping young adolescents' education and determining their attitudes and readiness for school learning as well as the fund of general knowledge they possess about life, the family, and the surrounding culture. In this section a chapter is devoted to each context, but it needs to be pointed out that these areas interact and influence one another just as do the domains of their personal development. ▪

Service learning projects provide meaningful community-based learning experiences.

6.
The Family

As young adolescents grow and mature, they find it necessary to interact harmoniously with many different people in a variety of settings. None of these settings is more complex than the family where intimate relationships inevitably change. As youngsters move into adolescence, their own maturation, coupled with the midlife changes of their parents, transform the dynamics of the entire family. Parents often view themselves as playing a diminished role in their children's lives as adolescents seek and gain more independence and autonomy. While the role of parents does change, young adolescents still need and really want parental involvement in their lives, albeit from a distance.

Parents are a child's first and best teachers; as children naturally acquire most of the beliefs, attitudes, and values held by their parents. As adolescents mature, however, they frequently question many of the beliefs. While teens often challenge or temporarily abandon the values and lifestyle modeled for them by their parents, when they emerge from adolescence they find that their views and behaviors are strikingly similar to those of their parents. This adds credence to the adage that the "apple does not fall far from the tree."

Responsible parents continue to monitor the activities and whereabouts of their young teens. Asking where they are going, who they will be with, and what kind of adult supervision will be provided are all legitimate questions to ask young adolescents when they plan to be away from home. Monitoring their in-house activities is also important. Parents should be aware of the television programs, video games, Internet sites, compact discs, and rental movies accessed by their children.

Besides being teachers, parents are also the providers for young adolescents. Raising a teen is an expensive proposition, especially when young adolescents view their parents as a limitless ATM machine. Parents need to use discretion in allotting family resources to meet the needs and wants of their teenagers. Parents also need to guide and support their children's activities. There are times when parents need to take a firm stand and tell their teens "no!" As discussed in Chapter 2, parents frequently need to function as a surrogate prefrontal cortex, since many young adolescents are not capable of consistently making wise decisions. Insisting that my 14-year-old wear his helmet when riding his bicycle is wise despite his protest that the helmet looks "stupid." Mature adult judgment should always override the sometimes naïve and idealistic opinions of young adolescents when their safety and well-being are at stake.

Parenting styles

Over time, experts in psychology and child development have sought the ideal model for parents to emulate while raising the next generation of competent and well-adjusted adults. One of the most accepted models of parenting was proposed by Diana Baumrind (1991) who described four styles of parenting: authoritative, authoritarian, permissive, and neglectful, each of which is associated with cultivating specific adolescent behaviors as outlined below.

Authoritative parenting style. While the perfect recipe for raising healthy, caring, competent, and well-adjusted adolescents does not exist, the authoritative model of parenting is very compatible with the nature and needs of young adolescents. This mode of parenting provides high levels of support for the developing adolescent but also holds the child accountable for her actions and decisions. While firm and clear limits and expectations are held for the child, those parameters are set for the young adolescent via discussion and negotiation. Baumrind (1991) characterized authoritative parenting by these traits:

- Communication—Open and honest discussion between parents and children is the norm.
- Expectations—Clear and realistic expectations are negotiated.
- Respect—Parents and children treat each other in a courteous and respectful manner.
- Affection—Warmth and closeness is evident in the home. (p. 62)

Authoritarian parenting style. The authoritarian mode of parenting is characterized by adult control. House rules that govern adolescents' behavior and habits are set unilaterally by parents. No input or compromise is sought or considered when setting limits or expectations. Communication between authoritarian parents and their young adolescent child is top-down and one-sided, with no bending or compromise concerning the strict rules by which their teen must abide. Infractions are dealt with harshly and in a punitive manner. Leniency is not practiced. Such parents might make such statements as, "As long as you live in my house, you will live by my rules!" or "It's my way or the highway!"

The authoritarian model of parenting does not promote healthy parent-child relationships nor does it promote positive adolescent behaviors. Young teens raised in authoritarian homes often lack the ability to make good decisions and think critically because they have had little opportunity to practice such skills. When parents communicate to their young adolescents in authoritarian ways, they discourage exploration and initiative.

Permissive parenting style. There are two types of indulgent parents—the permissive indulgent and the permissive indifferent. Both are characterized by little control or restrictions placed on their children. In this mode of parenting, the child is viewed as infallible and can do no wrong. Since the young adolescent has seldom heard the word "no," he is used to getting his own way and becomes self-centered. Permissive indulgent parents are highly supportive of their children but seldom hold their offspring accountable when they make poor choices and behave inappropriately. In fact, many indulgent parents actively deny that their son or daughter is capable of boorish behavior.

Permissive indifferent parents also exercise little control over their young teens, placing few, if any, restrictions on their activities. But unlike their permissive indulgent counterparts, indifferent parents exhibit little support for their child. Youngsters are allowed to come and go as they please and do as they wish so long as their activities do not inconvenience their parents in any way. Such parents might say to their children, "I don't care what you do, just don't expect me to bail you out if you get into trouble." This attitude toward parenting sends the message to young teens that one's behavior does not matter.

Regardless of the type of permissive style of parenting employed, the result is usually a child who exercises poor self-control. When youngsters raised in permissive families are placed in settings, such as school, where they are expected to follow rules and regulate their own behavior, they often find themselves at odds with adults in charge—unfortunate, but not surprising, since they have had no experience in conducting themselves within defined parameters.

Neglectful parenting style. I am not sure that one should dignify this type of parenting as a style. But, unfortunately, neglectful parenting does exist. Neglectful parents are aloof and disengaged from their children. They do not monitor their teens whereabouts, could not name their children's friends, nor are they involved in or actively supportive of any of their children's cocurricular activities. Children raised by neglectful parents have strong reasons to doubt that their parents really love and care about them. Since the adults who should care for them the most show little interest in their well-being, young adolescents reared in such an atmosphere become distrustful of adults. Neglectful parenting usually results in young adolescents who have poor social skills, handle independence poorly, and lack self-control. Many cases of neglectful parenting come close to being child abuse.

The case for authoritative parenting

Much evidence exists that supports the tenet that authoritative parenting is the best way to rear healthy, successful, and competent young adolescents and teens (Steinberg, 2001). Young adolescents raised by authoritative parents tend to develop a stronger sense of self-adequacy and self-concept compared to those raised under authoritarian or permissive parents. Children raised in an authoritative home are more independent and feel competent in the shaping of their own lives. Youngsters from authoritative homes, as you would expect, exhibit higher levels of academic achievement and success (Aunola, Stattin, & Nurmi, 2000). Even health and wellness issues are related to parenting style; tobacco use has been less prevalent among teens who experience high levels of authoritative parenting (Adamczyk-Robinette, Fletcher, & Wright, 2002). Children raised in authoritative homes are more receptive to the views and opinions of their parents compared to teens reared under other models of parenting (Arnold, Mackey, & Pratt, 2001).

Santrock (2005) summed up the findings of several recent studies concerning the good fit between authoritative parenting and meeting the needs of adolescents:

- Authoritative parents establish an appropriate balance between control and autonomy, giving adolescents opportunities to develop independence while providing the standards, limits, and guidance that adolescents need.
- Authoritative parents are more likely to engage adolescents in verbal give-and-take and allow adolescents to express their own views. Such compromises help youngsters build communication skills that are important in becoming socially competent individuals.
- The warmth and parental involvement provided by authoritative parents makes the adolescent more receptive to parental influences.

(p. 268)

While the authoritative model of parenting is recognized as the most effective style for raising well-adjusted youngsters, few parents exclusively operate from the authoritative mode. Often it is necessary to become authoritarian; or parents, if physically or emotionally exhausted, may slip into the indifferent quadrant when they are too spent to face issues presented by young adolescents. Flight attendants instruct passengers boarding airliners that, in case of a loss of cabin pressure, adults should put on their own oxygen masks first before attempting to help their children or others needing assistance. While the natural inclination of parents would be to help their children first, even at the expense of their own well-being, the wisdom of this instruction is clear. One can be of no assistance to others if incapacitated. Therefore, parents need to guard and protect their own personal well-being to be an effective resource for their young teens.

Young adolescents and the family in flux

As a middle school teacher, I often had discussions with parents concerning changes in their children's moods and behavior. The changes they noticed were likely the result of several factors working together that alter the dynamics of a home.

One of those factors is the onset of puberty. As a youngster matures, the metamorphosis brings with it changes in the dynamics of how children and parents relate to each other. The youngster is no longer a little boy or girl but is becoming a young man or woman, which will result in changes in behavior for both parents and child. For example, a father may feel reluctant to invite his young adolescent daughter to sit on his lap as she did as a child. Mothers may refrain from hugging their sons, fearing that this sign of affection may not be wanted. As a youngster, I recall numerous bouts of wrestling and rough housing on the living room floor with my father. My dad was always careful not to injure his young son. But one day, when I was about 14 years old, I pinned my father's shoulders to the floor. My dad realized that my physical strength equaled his own. We never wrestled again. It is important that parents and their young teen children understand such episodes for what they are—signs of a maturing family and not a decline in the love and affection among family members. The feelings of closeness and affection still need to be expressed but now in more age-appropriate ways.

Not only are young adolescents maturing physically but their intellectual abilities are no longer those of a child. Young adolescents' thinking abilities become more abstract and adult-like. They are capable of grappling intellectually with their parents and other adults on nearly equal ground. They are able to formulate logical arguments and points of view that do not always coincide with views of the parent. This often catches parents off guard as they have grown accustomed to winning arguments with their children. Parents may find it unsettling to have their child as an intellectual peer, and many claim that their young teen has become more argumentative. While it may be true that verbal confrontations are more common than before, young adolescents frequently engage parents and other adults in such arguments to practice their newfound intellectual ability and to clarify their own thinking. While few people enjoy arguments, parents and other adults working with young adolescents should recognize this trait as a sign of intellectual maturation rather than teens being intentionally difficult. As is true with any new skill, it takes practice to become proficient. While young adolescents begin to develop the cognitive skills to formulate complex arguments, they may lack the tact and social skills to express their ideas in a respectful manner. Parents, teachers, and other adults should listen closely to the ideas of young adolescents and try not to feel attacked or offended by an immature presentation. Caring adults can help young adolescents learn to present their positions in ways that will enhance rather than stifle communication.

HOW SHOULD I RESPOND?

A letter from school informs you that your 13-year-old son and his friends have been sprinkling their conversations with foul and vulgar language. As an authoritative parent, how would you address this situation?

1. Let your son know that his speech is not acceptable and ground him for a week.
2. Contact the school and let the administration know that your son has never used bad language in your presence and you don't think he would do such a thing at school.
3. Ask for your son's version of the episode and work together for a resolution to the situation.
4. Instruct your son to watch his language and be sure he is out of earshot of teachers if he chooses to use questionable language again.
5. Ignore the letter since "kids will be kids."
6. Other _____

Comment:

Authoritative parents know that young adolescents will make mistakes—that is part of growing up. You should invite dialogue about this situation and seek an opportunity to reach a mutual agreement to rectify the problem. Reasonable and appropriate consequences for future infractions should be made clear. This is a problem to be solved—How will the son change his behavior? Will he remove himself from the group? Will he apologize for his actions? In reviewing the options above, the reader should be able to identify responses more typical of authoritarian, indulgent, or neglectful parents.

Parents usually notice a change in their child's opinion of them as the youngster moves into the teen years. Most children hold an exalted view of their parents. They see them as brilliant, infallible, and perfect in every way. But when those same children reach early adolescence, the parents suddenly become stupid, inept, and flawed. Such a rapid fall from grace can be unsettling, even hurtful, for parents. So it is important for parents to understand that the demotion is not a personal attack but a response to the young teen's growing intellectual ability. Steinberg (1994) labeled this phenomenon *deidealization.* Young adolescents aspire to be adults and their parents are the most visible models they have for this revered life stage. Young adolescents have matured intellectually to the point that they realize that perfection is impossible to attain. As long as they view their parents as perfect people, becoming an adult is seen as an insurmountable task. So young teens often will look for flaws in their parents and seem to be delighted when the parents make a mistake or do something foolish. Young adolescents will frequently make uncomplimentary comments about the ineptness they have observed. Deidealization is not a personal attack but an attempt on the part of the child to make attaining adulthood a less daunting endeavor.

Young teens often will look for flaws in their parents and seem to be delighted when the parents make a mistake or do something foolish.

During early adolescence, most youngsters experience a transition from the elementary to the middle school setting, a change that can alter the dynamics of the family. More homework and school projects are required in middle school, calling for parents to adjust schedules and alter family routines. Transition to a middle school usually means that the school is farther from home. Longer commutes to the school may change morning routines. Participation in cocurricular activities may complicate transportation. Whatever the case, many parents find themselves chauffeuring their young adolescents to more places and over greater distances. The move to the middle school almost always widens the young adolescent's circle of friends; friends now live out of the neighborhood, and their families are not known by the parents.

Peers become increasingly more important, and young adolescents desire to spend more time with them. When young adolescents give family a lower priority, family relationships alter.

It is natural for parents to have goals and dreams for their children, and having positive expectations for them is healthy. But parents who predetermine important choices and attempt to live vicariously through their child often place their child in a difficult position. The classic example is the parent who plans a college or career choice for their child. But as the youngster matures, it becomes apparent that the path selected for him by the parents is in conflict with his own personal desires and talents. Such conflicting expectations can cause serious rifts in family relationships.

The young adolescent's desire for independence inevitably surfaces and is an issue that families need to negotiate. Young teens require some space and autonomy to function on their own. Parents are often a visual reminder that the young adolescent is still "a kid." When young adolescents are with their families in a public place, it is not unusual for the teen to walk several yards in front of or behind the family. Such separation is a statement that adult supervision is no longer required.

I vividly recall an episode that is a prime example of young adolescents' need for independence. I made it a tradition to reward students in my advisory group who earned honor roll status by treating them to lunch at a restaurant within walking distance of our school. I had grown accustomed to the pack of students walking a "safe distance" ahead of me to avoid giving the impression to any passers-by that they were under the watchful eye of an adult. One group, however, upon entering the restaurant asked if I would sit at a separate table. Honoring their request, we sat at different tables and I dined alone. Not long after we were seated, the county sheriff entered the restaurant and saw my students on a school day. He thought he had caught these students skipping school. Visually scanning the restaurant, he saw me seated alone at a corner booth. He knew that I was a teacher at the middle school. I nonverbally acknowledged that the students were with me. But the sheriff decided to have some fun with this situation. He strolled up to the students and asked them gruffly why they were not in school. They immediately pointed in my direction and simultaneously rushed to my table and sat as close to me as possible. I looked at the sheriff and declared that I had never seen any of those kids in my life. The look on my students' faces reaffirmed that while they want, need, and deserve some independence, they still desire an adult safety net when trouble surfaces.

Parental changes that alter family relationships

Parents generally are quick to note the transformations occurring in their young adolescent children which bring about changes in the dynamics of the family. But parents are usually not as attuned to developmental changes in their own lives that may create family discord as well.

By the time their children become teenagers, parents are dealing with their own midlife issues. Frequently parents are evaluating their own career choices and making changes that lead to relocating the family. This means that young teens are uprooted from friends and a social structure that is important to them. Marital dissatisfaction often seems to peak at this age, and divorce is common. The complexity of living in a one-parent or blended family frequently becomes a reality for many young adolescents.

Parents of young adolescents are often faced with financial strain. Raising young teens is an expensive proposition. Keeping them fed and clothed takes a larger chunk of the family budget than before. The refrigerator and pantry need restocking more frequently. Rapid growth spurts require shoes, shirts, and jeans to be replaced long before they are worn out. And the clothing for young adolescents often needs to bear the teen-sanctioned label of approval in order to be acceptable. The wide variety of valuable learning experiences now available in cocurricular activities often involve expensive travel.

Adults at midlife are sometimes referred to as the "sandwich generation"—caught between raising young adolescent children and caring for their own aging parents. The physical and emotional demands of caregiving for two generations on opposite ends of the developmental spectrum are considerable.

Adults at midlife are sometimes referred to as the "sandwich generation"—caught between raising young adolescent children and caring for their own aging parents.

As men and women approach midlife, they become aware that their physical strength and endurance are diminishing. My own father claimed that he knew he was getting older when it took him longer to rest up from physical exertion than it did to get tired—and now I know exactly what he meant. Some midlifers feel that life has passed them by and they have to deal with the reality that they have little chance of attaining some life goals set during their youth. Sometimes having a young adolescent living in the home is a constant reminder to parents of lost chances or a misspent youth. The phrase "midlife crisis" is often used to refer to the strange behavior exhibited by some middle-aged adults who try to recapture their lost youth. Spending a chunk of the college fund established for the young adolescent on a shiny new sports car is an example of how a "midlife crisis" can disrupt family relationships.

Adolescent and parent conflict

Even in families that enjoy a harmonious relationship between parents and young adolescent children, conflicts will occur. With most animal species, parents separate from or drive off their offspring when the progeny approach sexual maturity. But with humans, parents and physically mature children continue to live under the same roof for several years. It is, therefore, not surprising that conflicts will arise between parents and their maturing adolescents.

Dacey and Kenny (1997) reported that only about 25 percent of adolescents and their parents have frequent disputes; but even in such families trivial differences occur. When most adults think back to arguments they had with their parents when they were young adolescents, they generally recall issues about clothing, grooming, chores, cleaning one's room, choice and volume of music, and bedtime hours as major points of conflict. When viewed in the larger scheme of things, such issues are of little significance. Smetana, Yau, Restrepo, and Braeges (1991) found that working through conflicts with parents in a non-threatening and accepting family environment actually aided adolescents in developing positive interpersonal skills and independent thinking. Minor conflict between parents and their young adolescent children is a normal, natural, and even necessary part of development.

Resolving parent and young adolescent conflicts

While few people enjoy conflict and turmoil in the home, knowing that conflicts between young adolescents and parents is a by-product of the evolving family can be reassuring to both parents and their children. Steinberg (1994) proposed a method of collaborative problem solving that proves useful in resolving parent-adolescent conflicts in a respectful manner. His six point plan is summarized below:

- Establish ground rules for "fighting fair." At some point when no conflict is brewing, parents and young adolescents should establish a set of rules to govern the next confrontation when it arises.
- Parents and young adolescents should reach a mutual understanding of the problem with both parties sharing their perspective on the issue at hand.
- Brainstorm all possible solutions to the problem.
- Both parties select a solution they can support.
- Reach a consensus on a final resolution and record the final agreement.
- Have a follow-up discussion to monitor progress and success of the resolution. (pp. 249-253)

In some cases, parents may find it necessary to hand down an authoritarian decision to protect the safety or well-being of young teens. If an agreement cannot be reached via a collaborative process such as the one described above, young adolescents are more likely to comply with adult directives if they feel their positions are heard, thoughtfully considered, and taken seriously.

In summary

The only thing more difficult than parenting a young adolescent is being one. Early adolescence inevitably is a difficult and confusing life stage. To navigate it, they want, and secretly need, significant adults in their lives to assist them in the daunting task of growing up. ▪

7.
The Contemporary Society

To reword a famous literary expression by Charles Dickens, *Now is the best of times and the worst of times to be a young adolescent in the United States.* The opportunities that exist for young people today are amazing. Two summers ago my son spent three weeks touring Australia with 30 other young adolescents from northern New England. Last summer he traveled to the Netherlands to compete in an international baseball tournament. And every reader probably knows of similar overseas adventures of young adolescents. While many opportunities do exist for youth today, they live in a world that has so many out-of-school activities, they rarely have time just to be a kid. And media messages and advertisements encourage them to adopt behaviors and attitudes that are beyond their years. In *The Hurried Child,* David Elkind (1991) effectively captured the plight of young adolescents as they are hustled through childhood and early adolescence to accept adult-like expectations and experiences. Young adolescents are becoming seemingly more sophisticated compared to earlier generations; yet they lack the emotional maturity and wisdom to cope successfully with compromising situations in which their advanced worldly knowledge can place them. Some less advantaged young adolescents face serious problems associated with poverty, violence, and a lack of adult advocacy and guidance. Few adults would willingly trade places with young adolescents today. Growing up has never been easy, but today's society makes the task even more challenging.

Historical perspective of adolescence

The status of adolescence as a unique life stage has been frequently debated. For many, the notion that 10- to 15-year-olds are distinctly different from older adolescents and younger children is a hard sell. During the Civil War, young teens often fought beside adult soldiers. For many generations, youngsters worked in the fields, mines, and factories doing the same work as adult laborers. Many people married while still teenagers. Over a hundred years ago, the concept of juvenile justice did not exist, and teens were treated as adults for violations of criminal law. The concept of "teenager" did not exist. Those who did acknowledge differences between adolescents and adults did not always agree on the criteria that separated the life stages. The *inventionist view* (Santrock, 2005) of adolescence, for example, claimed that this life stage was a socioeconomic fabrication, rather than a function of human development, that kept youngsters out of jobs that could be held by adults. From the inventionist perspective, the child labor laws and compulsory education legislation that were enacted in this country during the early part of the twentieth century had more to do with warehousing youth and managing the economy than protecting minors.

Current reality

Our culture has created a situation in which it is difficult for young adolescents to find a niche. Few places exist in our society for young adolescents to fit in or contribute. Young adolescents complain that they are either "too young or too old" to engage in meaningful activities. When our country was predominately rural, young adolescents were desperately needed to work on the family farm. Schools in our country's corn belt even into the 1960s, excused absences for farm kids needed at planting and harvest times. Today's young adolescents are frequently excluded from genuine involvement due to mechanization that precludes the need for manual labor or their perceived immaturity, which inhibits adults from assigning them significant roles. This is why developmentally responsive middle level schools and the adults close to them work to find legitimate ways to engage young adolescents in meaningful activities.

Stereotyping young adolescents

Throughout history adolescents generally have been portrayed in a negative light. Many early Greek writers, Sophocles and Aristotle in particular, described adolescents of their time as self-absorbed, selfish, rude, impulsive, and disrespectful to their elders (Dacey & Kenny, 1997). Centuries later that perception of adolescents has changed very little. Adults report that they do not trust adolescents (Rice, 1996) and that they become uncomfortable when approached by a group of teens who are just "hanging out" in public places such as shopping malls (Matthews, Taylor, Percy-Smith, & Limb, 2000). When asked to describe teens today, many adults characterize them in disparaging terms. Such derogatory opinions are frequently derived from a highly visible minority of this age group who do get involved in delinquent behavior. The media are notorious for publicizing misdeeds of youth but are slow to report their positive work and involvement on many fronts. Such negative stereotypes about young adolescents are even more likely to take root if adults have little or no direct contact with them. Once negative stereotypes have formed they are difficult to refute. But research has found that when 11-,

12-, and 13-year-olds were brought together with adults and participated in joint activities, the attitudes of both generations toward each other greatly improved (Meshel, 2004). Such findings indicate that parents, schools, and organizations that serve young adolescents should do all they can to promote positive intergenerational contacts.

Social policy and young adolescents

The population of our nation is aging. As our population matures, social policy becomes slanted toward programs that benefit the older generation, since adults and the elderly comprise a huge voting block. The lion's share of government-sponsored social programs and resources is allocated to adults and senior citizens. The resulting fewer resources available for government programs to assist youth lead to a condition referred to as *generational inequity* (Santrock, 2005).

It has often been said that the future of any nation rests in the potential of its young people. For that reason, advocates for adolescents need to be active in pressing decision makers at all levels to ensure that teens are supported by policies and programs that will enhance their development. Resources allocated to benefit teens should be viewed as sound investments in the future rather than a drain on tax dollars. It is too easy to let the "bottom line" dictate decisions and policy impacting young people. Whether skate parks or schools, when communities propose spending money for youngsters, there is always a contingent opposed to the expenditure. While frugality and prudent use of limited resources is wise, not providing our young people with adequate resources to help them thrive and reach their full potential is shortsighted. The next generation of responsible adults is enrolled in our middle schools today; so is the next generation of criminals and felons. In Vermont, taxpayers spent about $27,000 in the year 2000 to house each inmate incarcerated through the Vermont Department of Corrections (Hogan & Murphy, 2000), while in 2005 we allocated about $8,700 to educate each child

The next generation of responsible adults is enrolled in our middle schools today.

(Vermont Department of Education, 2005). Nationally, the costs are very similar, with incarceration costing 50 to 75 percent more than states allocate for educating each youngster (U.S. Department of Justice, 2002). The moral is that it is much more cost effective to invest now in tomorrow's future by educating young adolescents and keeping them in school, than it is to rehabilitate young people gone astray.

A major responsibility of being a middle level educator is to be an advocate for young adolescents, a group that wields almost no political clout. Therefore, it is necessary for adults who work with them and their parents to push for legislation, programs, and resources that will help young people maximize their full potential.

Young adolescents and the media

In the last 50 years, the proliferation of media has soared in this country and around the world. As a young child, I recall walking two blocks to my grandparents' house to watch cartoons on Saturday morning because my family did not own a television set. My experience was not unusual in the early 1950s. Now most families have multiple color sets accompanied by other forms of media to keep us hooked up, wired, connected, and online. Santrock (2005) reported the average American teen lives in a home that has three television sets, three audio tape players, three radios, two VCRs, two CD players, one video game player, and one computer. Over two-thirds of adolescents have a television in their bedrooms while 20 percent have a private computer. Cellular phones have become almost standard equipment in middle schoolers' backpacks. Nine out of ten 12- to 15-year-olds are frequent users of the Internet (Keith & Martin, 2005). But Ishizuka (2005) cautioned not to use technology as another way to pigeonhole and stereotype teens, since many young adolescents are often more savvy about the use of technology and online resources than adults.

Role of media for young adolescents

Young adolescents use media and technology for many purposes. Arnett (1995) identified five categories of reasons why adolescents access media.

- Entertainment—A pleasurable way to spend leisure time.
- Identity formation—Adolescents assume a variety of roles in the media. A part of identity formation is deciding what kind of individual one would like to become. Young teens can try on several possible identities vicariously through teen characters played out in movies and television. Gender role identity can be explored through many forms of media.
- High sensation—Young adolescents have a strong desire to have their senses intensely stimulated. Loud music, thrilling rides at amusement parks, and horror movies fulfill this desire.
- Coping—Young teens use the media as a way to relax and escape from the frustrations of real life.
- Youth culture identification—By being well acquainted with the latest movie, CD, Web site, or television program that is popular with peers, young adolescents can use media as a means of gaining acceptance with their age mates. Much of the vocabulary, speech patterns, fashion, and values of teens are conveyed via the media. The media also "standardizes" youth culture, making the latest teen trend fashionable from coast to coast.

The Carnegie Council on Adolescent Development (1996) made the following statement that is even more true now that when it was written:

> The adolescent's world cannot be understood without considering the enormous power of the mass media, especially television, but also movies and popular music. Together with the increasing penetration of cable television, videocassette recorders, and computers in American homes and schools, these electronic conduits for programming and advertising have become strong competitors to the traditional societal institutions in shaping young people's attitudes and values. (p. 41)

The next sections examine specific forms of media and how they impact the lives of young adolescents.

Young adolescents and television

Television, for both good and bad, has a tremendous impact on young people. Studies reveal young people annually spend more of their waking hours watching television than any other single activity (Jones, 2004). Studies have shown that television viewing habits and the amount of parental monitoring and restrictions placed on television use by their teenage children serve as a predictor of how their child's use of other media is regulated (Roberts, Foehr, Rideout, & Brodie, 2005). The negative and debilitating effects of excessive television viewing by young teens are well documented. Attention deficits, poor decision making, decline in academic skills (especially reading), overly aggressive

Young people annually spend more of their waking hours watching television than any other single activity.

behavior, decline in self-esteem, obesity, and social isolation have all been linked to excessive television viewing (Carnegie Council on Adolescent Development, 1996). Television viewing also provides young teens with a distorted view of reality. Values and attitudes commonly portrayed on network and cable TV could easily be construed as cultural norms that set the parameters for acceptable behavior in our society. Complex problems are easily solved, permanent consequences of violence, and long-term repercussions for poor choices are seldom portrayed on TV drama. Perpetuation of ethnic and racial stereotypes also has been associated with television viewing.

Television has many redeeming qualities. It offers a world view of different cultures, customs, and beliefs, and can be a resource to promote peace and global understanding. There are some TV specials and documentaries that send positive and uplifting messages as well as provide quality entertainment, but these are merely the exception, not the rule.

Young adolescents and movies

Going to the movies when I was a youngster meant driving 25 miles to the nearest city to view the latest release on the big screen. Now, movies are purchased or rented on CDs or tapes for viewing at home. Yet, for young adolescents, going to the movies is still a favorite pastime. The feature film playing is of less importance than the opportunity to congregate with friends. Parents, of course, need to be concerned about the content of movies to be viewed.

What is worrisome about the content of television programs also applies to movies, but even more so. Greenberg, Siemicki, and Dorfman (1986) found that movies intended for mature audiences (R-rated) contained seven times more sexual content compared to television. While it is true that a complex rating system is intended to prohibit youngsters from viewing questionable material, evidence suggests the rating system is ineffective or may even be counterproductive. Bushman and Cantor (2003) found restrictive media ratings made them more appealing and attractive to children as young as eight years of age. It is no secret that many young people find ways to view R- or even X-rated movies. When inquisitive youth see material intended for mature audiences, they come away with a warped sense of adult behavior. Even movies that are deemed suitable for young adolescent audiences (PG-13) often portray male and female characters and their relationships in ways that are less than wholesome. At a time when young adolescents have a natural interest in forming romantic relationships, most rational adults would not want their children to adopt their sexual scripts from those portrayed by the visual media.

It is no secret that many young people find ways to view R- or even X-rated movies.

Young adolescents and music

As youngsters mature, their leisure time media use becomes more auditory including iPods and MP3 players, compact discs, tapes, and radio (Roberts & Foehr, 2004). Each adult generation concludes that music will be the ruination of youth. Adults in the 50s were appalled at the music and gyrations of Elvis Presley. The popularity of shaggy-haired musicians and acid rock music spelled trouble for youngsters in the 60s and 70s. Presently, the same concern over the eroding impact of today's popular music, rap, and heavy metal is equally unsettling for adults.

Adults typically are concerned about the messages young adolescents take away from listening to contemporary music, regardless of the decade. Much of today's music is available to young consumers in video format, a genre made popular by MTV more than 20 years ago. Music videos often are classified as *concept videos*, which portray a vivid scenario as told by the lyrics of the song. Many of the concept videos are steeped in sexual acts, drug use, and violence. Rap videos today frequently represent men as violent, sexist, and abusive to women. Females frequently are presented as sex objects and subjects of exploitation. Heavy metal music has a reputation for being depressing and dark. Lawsuits have been filed against musicians by parents whose teen children committed suicide after listening to a steady diet of heavy metal music (Arnett, 2004).

While not all rap and heavy metal music is controversial, much of it does contain offensive lyrics—at least to adults. It is easy to conclude that impressionable teens would be influenced by what they see and hear in such videos. But studies reveal that when experiencing the same music video, adults and young adolescents have different interpretations about what they see and hear (Werner-Wilson, Fitzharris, & Morrissey, 2004). There is evidence that even teens themselves interpret differently the messages sent via concept music videos depending on sex and race of the individual (Brown & Schulze, 1990). The few studies that have tried to link young teen music preferences to unhealthy or antisocial behavior have shown correlations between them but no clear cause-and-effect associations (Strasburger & Wilson, 2002).

Young adolescents and the electronic age

In the last few years, new forms of media and technology have burst upon the scene. No other innovations have had a greater impact on how we live in today's electronic age than recent advances in technology. Computers are now everywhere, including classrooms, and are integrated into our daily lives at a rapid rate. The Internet, e-mail, instant messaging, and video games are among the new technological advances popular with today's young adolescents.

The Internet, instant messaging, and blogs. The Internet is very popular among young adolescents, with about 65 percent of 10- to 13-year-olds reporting they use the Internet frequently, and about one in two report "surfing the net" daily (Kaiser Family Foundation, 2002). Adolescents use the Internet to gather general information, do research for school projects, and communicate with friends via e-mail and chat rooms. As adolescent online time increased, adults speculated that boys and girls would make gender specific use of the medium. Boys were expected to spend more time online than girls. Boys were expected to randomly surf the Web and play video games, while girls were projected to spend time shopping and chatting online. Data collected by self-disclosure surveys, however, reveal that young teens use the Internet in strikingly similar ways, regardless of gender (Gross, 2004).

Since its advent in 1998, instant messaging (IM) has become immensely popular among middle school students. Nearly 13 million teens report using IM services frequently, and one in five claims it is the major way that they keep in touch with friends (Lenhart, Rainie, & Lewis, 2002). Since their social agenda is a top priority for most 10- to 15-year-olds, instant messaging provides them with a new way to communicate with peers. The telephone has served that function for decades and still does. But many IM services offer features that trump the telephone. While each IM conversation is carried on between two parties, young adolescents frequently maintain three or more online chats simultaneously. IM users can exchange files or send hyperlinks and pictures through many IM services. Not only does IM allow for instant communication among young teens who spend time together every day, but it is just as easy to contact peers who live anywhere in the world. Using instant messaging and being included on a popular "buddy list" of the cool crowd is a means for young adolescents to earn status and gain social acceptance among peers (Kastner & Wyatt, 2004). Instant messaging also provides young adolescents a sense of power and autonomy. They have devised acronyms and online lingo to communicate via IM that make many online conversations nearly indecipherable to the prying eyes of adults.

Another feature of the Internet that has recently surfaced is the *blog*, a term that is derived from the word Weblog. A blog is essentially an online journal through which individuals can post thoughts about a specific topic and have others respond to their ideas. Audio and video messages, as well as hyperlinks and pictures can be sent via blogs. Teachers are beginning to tap the interactive potential of blogs for educational purposes (Renard, 2005).

The Internet and its associated features (e-mail, instant messaging, and blogs), while they hold much promise for education, also present new problems and genuine dangers to young adolescents. This is particularly true since many young teens possess much more "cyber sense" than the adults charged with monitoring their well-being. Most frightening is the presence of sexual predators who frequently scan the Internet looking for young victims. A survey of 10- to 17-year-olds who were frequent users of the Internet found that 20 percent had received online requests for sexual contact (Finkelhor, Mitchell, & Wolak, 2000). Page and Page (2003) designed these guidelines to help protect vulnerable teens from online solicitation:

- Before subscribing to any online services, establish ground rules.
- Locate computers used by teens in high-traffic areas in the home.
- Never give out personal information online.

- Never agree to a face-to-face meeting with online acquaintances, especially if it is suggested that the meeting be private.
- Do not respond to offensive or suspicious online communications.
- Turn off the computer immediately if a pornographic site is accessed accidentally. Simply pressing the escape key is ineffective on many such sites and will activate other offensive sites. (pp. 92–93)

WHO IS RESPONSIBLE?

Mr. Black is not very computer savvy, but he recognizes the power of online learning and the extensive resources available on the Internet. A major concern is that his students not use their computer time to play electronic games or visit inappropriate Web sites. What should Mr. Black do to allow his students access to technology, not use it inappropriately?

1. Place all monitors so they can be easily seen by adults.
2. Install filters to limit access to inappropriate sites.
3. Ask students to promise to use technology only for the intended purpose.
4. Work with students so they understand their responsibilities when having access to the Internet.
5. Other _____

Comment:

This is a teachable moment. Since the World Wide Web is totally accessible to anyone unless blocked by filters, teachers need to ensure that online time is productive and spent for the purpose intended. Most schools have developed an Acceptable Use Policy that spells out the expectations for proper use of technology. Individual teachers are encouraged to set their own classroom guidelines. Students and parents could also sign a document that verifies each student knows the rules and understands the consequences of noncompliance. One idea that would appeal to middle level students is to issue an "Internet Driver's License" when they agree to abide by the established rules. If the guidelines are violated, the student's license is revoked for a specified period of time (Cotton, 2000).

Teen use of technology presents problems that require adult monitoring and supervision. Online time often competes with other responsibilities such as homework and chores. Excessive time online or in front of a computer can lead to social isolation, leaving less time to spend with friends and family. Gossip and rumors spread quickly online, and pranks can quickly get out of hand. Cyber-bullying can be brutal because verbal attacks are often bolder than they would be in a face-to-face encounter (Kastner & Wyatt, 2004). Like any other innovation, online technology can be a powerful tool for progress or an instrument of destruction. For many young adolescents, the presence of adult guidance will determine which function of technology will be realized.

Video games

While video and computer games seem to be relatively new inventions, they have been around for more than 30 years. Since the days of *Pong* and *Pac-Man*, video games have become more realistic and titillating making them extremely popular with young adolescents. Studies indicate that adolescents spend nearly eight hours per day engaged in the use of some sort of media (Roberts, Foehr, Rideout, & Brodie, 1999). This fact holds true for virtually all economic and ethnic groups in this country since three-quarters of teens from low-income families reported having access to cable television in their homes and 83 percent played video games on a regular basis. Computer use between European American and African American teens was reported as nearly equal while Hispanic young people reported slightly less time using technology (Roberts & Foehr, 2004).

Adolescents spend nearly eight hours per day engaged in the use of some sort of media.

As with the other types of popular media, much concern and attention has been focused on the impact of video games on the malleable minds of youth. Many of the negative messages sent to teens by television, music, and movies apply to video games as well. But compared to network television, video games are even more guilty of overt portrayal of violence, sexism, and racism (Berger, 2006). In many video games women are presented as victims or admiring fans of the male Caucasian hero. In 80 percent of video games the "winner" has to employ some form of violence or aggression to prevail (Dietz, 1998). In my mind, the video games industry certainly crossed another line of indecency by releasing a "game" that features graphic scenes of cannibalism (Miga, 2005). David Walsh (2001), president of the National Institute on Media and the Family, summarized his views in this statement: "The intense concern about video and computer games is based on the belief that the ultra violent games are inappropriate for all children and harmful for some" (http://culturalpolicy.uchicago.edu/conf2001/papers/walsh.html).

Yet, the direct impact of steeping young minds in the blood and gore of violent video games has been difficult to ascertain. Many studies have found only a correlation between frequent participation in video games and aggressive behavior. Research is fairly new in this arena, and more time is needed to complete longitudinal studies to determine long-term effects. Anderson and Bushman (2002) emphasized that the relationship between exposure to graphic video games and its link to behavior is very complex. As proposed in their General Aggression Model (GAM), Kooijmans (2004) succinctly summarized Anderson and Bushman's theory:

> Both situational and personal variables interact to affect a person's internal state. The internal state consists of cognition (thoughts), affect (feelings) and arousals (physical). All three of these items influence each other, and each has an effect on an individual's interpretation of an aggressive act. Once the brain's interpretation is complete, decision-making processes start to occur....Anderson and Bushman hypothesized that violent video games influence behavior by promoting aggressive beliefs and attitudes, thus creating aggressive schema, aggressive behavioral scripts, and aggressive expectations. They also claim that it desensitizes individuals to aggression. (www.personalityresearch. org/papers/kooijmans.html)

It is unlikely that the cause of violent and aggressive behavior will ever be isolated to a single factor. Yet it is difficult to imagine that media violence has little or no impact on behavior. Not all young adolescents who are exposed to unsavory scenes through the media will imitate what they witness. But couple media violence with other psychological factors, such as hostility, and it is not hard to imagine a young adolescent out of control and dangerous. Video games are more interactive than movies and television, putting the young teen in command of the action figures on screen. In order to win many video contests, the player must kill his opponent or an innocent victim, usually in a gruesome fashion. Taking this scenario a step further, simulations such as paint ball and laser tag require putting a human target in the sights of a weapon and pulling the trigger. This form of entertainment seems to cross the line between fantasy and reality.

To be fair, video games like all other forms of media have some positive values and redeeming qualities. Video games are often credited for improving players' hand-eye coordination, manual dexterity, and reaction time. Some video games take the form of puzzles that can be used for therapeutic purposes or to stimulate the mind. Video simulations can be used for educational or training purposes by the military, government, and business communities. Some recent simulations have replicated historical events, placing players in a scenario where planning, problem solving, and critical thinking skills are required. Young adolescents need to develop a sense of competency, and mastering a video game can provide a venue for achievement. While some feel that video games may be at least partially responsible for aggressive behavior in teens, others feel that such games may serve as an outlet for unexpressed anger in a form that will not physically harm others (Stupak, 2004).

Education and the electronic age

Students today have never known a time when the world was not dominated by technology, and this reality has changed the way students learn and think. Increasingly, students now learn in more visual modes. Going to the library to do research is not as common as it was. Students' experience and proficiency in using high-speed Internet services make, in their minds, searching printed references obsolete. Renard (2005) provided an example of the changing educational landscape from a secondary English as a Second Language (ESL) classroom. While students struggled with the English language, they were computer proficient. They found Web sites that would translate, define, and even pronounce unfamiliar words. They soon refused to consult traditional dictionaries because they were slow to use, tedious, and inefficient.

To keep pace with the technological inclinations of students in today's middle schools, educators are looking for ways to embrace rather than subvert technology to enhance learning. For many young people, the use of technology is a motivator and holds their attention for relatively long periods of time. According to Schaffer and his colleagues (2005), the producers of video games have tapped into powerful components of learning theory, which makes the virtual experience compelling for young learners. To master many video games, players need to understand the situation simulated on the screen and be able to apply knowledge and skills to be successful and move to more advanced levels of competition.

Educators should embrace the engaging power and higher-order thinking skills inherent in most video games and capture their potential for educational purposes.

Video game players communicate effectively with and compete against other "gamers," thereby creating virtual social relationships. Video games make it possible for young learners to try on new identities by participating in computer simulations. Finally, video games generally require the player to take on the qualities and disposition of the action figures they control on the monitor. Educators should embrace the engaging power and higher-order thinking skills inherent in most video games and capture their potential for educational purposes. They should produce video games in which "players learn biology by working as a surgeon, history by writing as a journalist, mathematics by designing buildings as an architect or engineer, geography by fighting as a soldier, or French by opening a restaurant. More precisely, these players learn by inhabiting virtual worlds based on the way surgeons, journalists, architects, soldiers, and restaurateurs develop their epistemic frames" (Schaffer, Squire, Halverson, & Gee, 2005, p. 108).

Other researchers corroborate these findings and add more reasons why young adolescents enjoy the challenge of mastering a difficult computer game but shy away from rigorous school assignments. According to Jenkins (2005), youngsters are intrinsically motivated to play video games for the reasons that also should encourage their learning in school:

- Video games pose no real threat of failure. There are no harsh consequences for not performing well. If mistakes are made, one can reboot the computer and try again.
- Video games actively engage the student and immerse her fully. Through video games, the player makes decisions and witnesses the consequences of the choices she makes. Via printed text the student merely interprets what is portrayed by the author.
- Electronic games are designed to encourage early success, thus stimulating the youngster to continue playing.
- Video games make learning indispensable to "winning" the game. Specific information is often needed and used to solve virtual problems posed in the game.
- Video game players develop a social network of peers who share their interest in the game. They frequently share experiences, tips, and knowledge, which fosters a sense of competency.
- Video games are multimodal and stimulate players' auditory and visual senses while requiring them to be involved kinesthetically.

(pp. 49–50)

The electronic age—bridging the gap

Young adolescents of the digital age are demanding their learning experiences at school be as exciting and challenging as the latest electronic innovation. Prensky (2006), calls today's students "digital natives" who learn to use technology with ease by being fully immersed in the electronic culture, while he calls most adults "digital immigrants," always behind the electronic learning curve. Prensky advises:

As educators, we must take our cues from our students' 21st century innovations and behaviors, abandoning, in many cases, our own pre-digital instincts and comfort zones. Teachers must practice putting engagement before content when teaching. They need to laugh at their own digital immigration accents, pay attention to how their students learn, and value and honor what their students know.... Teachers needn't master all the new technologies. They should continue what they do best: leading discussion in the classroom. But they must find ways to incorporate into those discussions the information and knowledge that their students acquire outside the classroom in their digital lives. (p. 10)

Middle level education has a long tradition of honoring student voice and valuing lifelong learning. By carefully observing how students learn via technology and encouraging the use of appropriate media and electronic power tools, we can engage students in meaningful learning. When adult educators attempt to improve their own technology skills, they model for their students the value and need for lifelong learning.

Young adolescents as consumers

Madison Avenue and corporate America pay attention to young people in the U. S.—and for good reason. The 32 million young people between 12 and 19 years of age in 2003 added $175 billion to corporate coffers through their discretionary spending (Pennington, 2004). Corporate marketing strategies target young teens because of their vulnerability to peer pressure and their need for conformity. Wearing the "right" brand of clothing or owning the latest digital device is a way for young adolescents to "fit in" and earn status among their peer group.

Educators and parents need to help young adolescents learn to be discerning about media they consume and the advertising to which they are exposed. Many middle level schools now incorporate media literacy into their curriculum. Encouraging young adolescents to analyze information they see and hear through various forms of media is developmentally appropriate. Ten- to 15-year-olds are seeking more autonomy and are curious about world events. Their heightened sense of justice makes them sensitive to inequities that are apparent through the media. Young adolescents pick up on the mixed messages they see and hear but need opportunities to process what they observe.

Commercialism in schools

Another sign that school age kids are a viable and profitable market for businesses and corporations to tap is the rise of commercialism in our nation's schools. According to the Council for Corporate and School Partnerships (Molnar, 2004), schools throughout the country receive about $2.4 billion annually from business contributions and sponsorships. As school budgets continue to rise and local tax dollars are stretched to meet expenses, school administrators become more receptive to seeking revenues from the private sector. Many schools and businesses have forged mutually beneficial partnerships. In exchange for monetary donations or resources to supplement schools' programs, corporations expect to profit from the relationship in one or more ways.

According to Molnar (2005), school and business partnerships fall into eight major categories:

- Sponsorships of programs and activities—Businesses will often sponsor scholarships or academic competitions.
- Exclusive agreements—Schools can grant exclusive rights to businesses to sell their products on school property for a substantial percentage of the revenue generated.
- Incentive programs—Companies will reward students who have shown good academic progress or citizenship with products or vouchers.
- Appropriation of space—Schools now sell advertising space in buildings, stadiums, and even buses. As in major league sports, some schools even sell the naming rights of auditoriums and gymnasiums to the highest bidder.
- Sponsorship of educational materials—Many corporations produce curricula related to their business or industry.
- Electronic marketing—Channel One is likely the best-known form of electronic marketing to students. In exchange for free video equipment for classrooms, teachers agree to allow their students to watch a 12-minute news report punctuated with two minutes of commercials promoting products that would be popular with young audiences. The use of the Internet in schools also exposes students to a plethora of products.
- Privatization—Some schools are being operated by for-profit school management firms. Also, one of the nation's largest shopping mall developers has partnered with schools to establish alternative "Educational Resource Centers" that actually hold school in shopping malls.
- Fund raising—What parent of a school-age child has not been subjected to a school fund raiser? In many programs, each child is expected to sell a quota of products and prizes are awarded to the best "salespersons" as incentive. In fund-raising programs, the school retains a percentage of the profits earned by the student-generated sales. (pp. 77–78)

While it is easy to see why school administrators may be attracted to corporate offers to help balance lean budgets, care must be taken to keep the welfare of students foremost in mind. Many school-business relationships can be mutually beneficial, but a school should develop a policy to ensure that any agreement forged with a corporate entity is consistent with the school mission and is in the best interest of students. What message would be sent if students learn in health class about the importance of a nutritious diet but the food court is dominated by fast food and vending machines filled with high-calorie soda?

CASE STUDY

WHAT IS THE DIFFERENCE BETWEEN NEEDS AND WANTS?

The start of a new school year loomed with Josh about to enter eighth grade. Since he had outgrown most of his school clothes from the previous year, a trip to the mall was in order. As Josh and his mom walked to the discount department store where they usually shopped, Josh informed his mother that he wanted to select his own clothes from other shops that carried designer labels and popular styles. She agreed to window shop. The thing that caught Josh's eye was a pair of sneakers that cost approximately 75 percent of the family budget allotted for Josh's back-to-school clothing. Josh was intent on buying that pair of shoes. What should his mother do?

1. Agree to buy the shoes since he wants them so badly.
2. Give Josh the amount of money that would have been spent on shoes and expect him to make up the difference from his allowance.
3. Insist that he select a pair of shoes from the discount store, along with the rest of his clothes.
4. With Josh's input, make a list of everything he needs, give Josh the money allotted for his clothing, and allow him to purchase his wardrobe. Then let him live with his choices.
5. Other _____

Comment

Parents must understand that young adolescents desperately need to "fit in" and be a part of the crowd. Wearing the right brand name and current fashion is a way to be accepted by peers. Yet, young teens must realize that their "needs" are often expensive and cannot be satisfied at the expense of the entire family. Wise parents will use opportunities such as this to teach the value of a dollar and how individuals need to discriminate between their "needs" and our "wants". Options 2 or 4 seem logical.

In summary

Being a young adolescent has always been a challenge. But in the twenty-first century, the growing up process has been made more complicated. Through media influence many young adolescents today are thrust into the adult world prematurely. Young teens face a daily media blitz that tells them how they should look, feel, dress, and speak. Recently, I attended a middle school basketball game. Two 14-year-old girls strolled into the gymnasium wearing very short mini-skirts and extremely high spike heals. I am confident that their wardrobe was not guided by common sense on a snowy, below zero evening in northern Vermont, but rather by what some fashion designers dictate as trendy. The tragedy of young teens' growing up too quickly is that they may miss the fun of just being a kid. Compared to adulthood, adolescence is a very brief period in the entire life span. Adults should do all they can to help young adolescents enjoy and get the most out of the limited middle level years. They are going to be adults for a very long time.

Technology has opened a whole new world of instant communication, information, and entertainment, which young adolescents find highly stimulating but with attendant dangers. Our technology-saturated society is changing the way the media generation learns and processes information. It is important for middle level teachers and parents to direct young adolescents' appetite for technology, using it to enhance their children's educational experiences. ■

As some young adolescents see it ...

We are not the reckless, irresponsible troublemakers
that the media makes us out to be.
Bradlee, age 14

I don't want to grow up too fast, but I feel like I am being
pressured into doing so.
Fiona, age 12

The worst part of being a teen today is dealing with
the unfair judgments and stereotypes people have about us.
Abby, age 12

THE WELL-BEING OF YOUNG ADOLESCENTS

The close relationship between one's physical health and learning is well established by research studies and common sense. Students with currently active physical problems simply don't make good learners. This is also true with those whose mental health is impaired by the stress or anxiety brought on by some personal problem. As long-time middle level advocate, Dick Lipka has often said, "Cognitive learning is hard-won by someone whose life is in affective disarray."

Especially for young adolescents, and most especially in our contemporary culture, growing up is a daunting task that is inevitably beset with health and wellness issues and challenges. In this last section, one chapter provides a quite comprehensive and detailed examination of many relevant topics ranging from nutrition to sex and most everything that falls in between. The second chapter focuses on prevention strategies and conditions. Parents and educators can do much to arm young adolescents for successfully surmounting the challenges they will face as they leave childhood far behind and ultimately arrive at the high school as healthy and positive adolescents. ▧

Increasingly, middle schools are actively promoting fitness.

8.
Health and Wellness Issues

From labor union halls to the chambers of Congress, health care has become a front burner issue. It is often said that one's health is a person's most valuable possession. Those of us who have been blessed with good health realize how precious it is when an accident or illness puts us on the sidelines. But young teens give little thought to guarding their health and safety; by nature, most of them are vigorous and relatively free from disease. Yet, their well-being is potentially threatened by two major factors, one developmental and one societal. Tending to think they are invulnerable to anything bad happening to them, they believe that health and safety hazards associated with risky behavior will not apply to them personally. Regrettably, the decisions teens ultimately make, frequently called "fateful choices," are currently being made at younger ages than they were for previous generations. Today's middle schoolers make decisions about substance use and sexual activity, choices most people of previous generations did not face until at least high school. The health-related decisions and habits established during the early teen years often have long-term or even permanent impact on one's well-being.

As with many other elements of their lives, young adolescents are frequently caught in an "in-between" stage when it comes to their physical and physiological welfare. There are over half a million practicing physicians in the United States but fewer than 200 specialize in adolescent medicine (FLETEL Business Services, 2005). Pediatricians, who are technically trained to serve patients up to 21 years of age, devote the bulk of their time serving infants and toddlers. General practitioners can treat teens but most of their practice is with adults and senior citizens. So young adolescents who are fortunate to have access to health care are generally served by physicians who have limited training and experience in adolescent health concerns or, just as important, know how to counsel with adolescent patients (Kantrowitz & Springen, 2005). Recently, I took my 14-year-old son to our family doctor for a physical examination so Casey could participate in his school's athletic program. When the

121

routine examination was completed, our doctor politely dismissed me to the waiting room so he could have some private time with my son. I was not privy to the consultation, nor did I pry. But I suspect their discussion centered on health and wellness issues that impact young teens. My wife and I have initiated such conversations with our son in the past. But a booster from his doctor, whom Casey admires and respects, was greatly appreciated. All young adolescents should be so fortunate!

The middle school philosophy since its inception has been committed to serving the "whole child." The original *Turning Points* (Carnegie Council on Adolescent Development, 1989) spelled out five qualities that all students should exhibit if they have been well-served by their middle school. The last, but certainly not the least important, of those qualities, is "a healthy person" (p. 15). In *Turning Points 2000* (Jackson & Davis, 2000*),* middle level experts continued to assert that the health and fitness of young adolescents are important links to student success. Educators intuitively know that students have difficulty learning if their physical and psychological needs have not been satisfied. Given the strong connection between students' health and their ability to learn, effective middle schools work diligently to help their students develop healthy lifestyles and do all they can to surround them with a safe learning environment.

Health and wellness issues that impact young adolescents

Few afflictions are unique to 10- to 15-year-olds, but many health and wellness concerns arise during the adolescent years with particular implications for this age group. Some of these health-related issues are discussed in the following sections.

Nutrition. It is hard to believe that we live in a land of plenty yet have so many people poorly fed. According to the U.S. Department of Agriculture (1994–1996), only 2 percent of school-age children eat the daily recommended servings from all five major food groups. This fact is particularly true for young adolescents. Many young teens overeat on unhealthy fast foods or are malnourished because they limit caloric intake. The pressure from society to maintain a slender figure is so great that many girls intentionally limit their food intake to the point where malnutrition is a concern. Not all students are undernourished by choice. There probably is not a public school in the nation without some students who qualify for free or reduced cost meals. According to the Vermont Department of Education Web site, one of the most affluent schools in the state reported 12 percent of its students applied for subsidized lunches during the 2004–2005 academic year. Hundreds of schools have half or more of the student body qualify for free or reduced price lunches. Many schools also offer breakfast and snack programs to help satisfy the nutritional requirements of growing bodies. This likely means that food served at school to students from low-income families may be the most nutritious meals those youngsters consume all day.

The implication of all this is that middle schools should do all they can to encourage healthy eating habits and ensure access to high-quality meals at school. But just because a school offers a lunch program does not guarantee that the meals consumed are nutritious. Providing foods that comply with government guidelines, and satisfy the taste buds of a finicky clientele is a tall order. Even if schools do offer a quality food service program, they may pit the school lunch program against alternatives that offer less healthy food choices. Snack bars, vending machines, and á la carte selections frequently vie for students' appetites. Reporting on the results of an extensive study of young adolescent eating habits in middle schools, Meyer and her colleagues (2004) reported that pizza, French fries, and chips were the most frequently purchased items in á la carte lines of the middle schools surveyed. From vending machines and school snack bars, students' most popular purchases were soda, candy, sports drinks, chips, cookies, and flavored water. Such results are consistent with the general observations that young adolescents' diets contain large amounts of fat and sugar.

Not only is the quality of food that young adolescents consume important to their well-being, but middle schools should also pay attention to other factors contributing to a healthy nutritional program. An attractive cafeteria, time to eat and socialize, pleasant staff, and a variety of menu items are all important elements to encourage middle schoolers to eat healthier diets at school.

At such a critical point in life when the body grows and develops rapidly, it is essential that young adolescents have access to nutritious food and establish healthy eating habits. Proper nutrition is the key to helping young adolescents reach their full developmental potential. While the family and society are important factors in developing the eating habits of youngsters, middle schools should do all that is within their sphere of influence to foster proper nutrition among their charges.

Proper nutrition is the key to helping young adolescents reach their full developmental potential.

Eating Disorders. Associated with adolescent nutrition are three common eating disorders—obesity, anorexia, and bulimia nervosa. Each of these complex problems carries serious health risks. While no simple solution exists to curb eating disorders that plague many young adolescents, caring adults can do much to help youngsters construct and maintain healthy eating habits.

Obesity. Gaining weight is generally a simple matter of supply and demand. Our bodies require a specific number of calories per day to grow, repair, and sustain themselves. Any additional calories consumed are stored by the body as fat. If an individual repeats this pattern over a long period of time, the extra body fat accumulates and the person becomes overweight. If the condition persists unchecked, the condition progresses to obesity.

The physiological reason for obesity is easy to understand, but controlling its onset is complex. Obesity used to be a problem that haunted adults. But in recent years, overweight youth have caused the medical profession to sound the alarm. Sixteen percent, or nearly nine million, school-age children and adolescents were classified as overweight two years ago (Buddy, 2005). In the last 25 years the number of overweight children has tripled, with poor nutrition and lack of exercise cited as the main culprits (Satcher, 2005). Eating out has become a common pastime for Americans; and fast food, high in both fat and calories, is popular with young people. Portion sizes at fast-food establishments have ballooned over the years. In 1957, the average fast-food hamburger weighed about one ounce. Now that same sandwich tips the scales at six ounces (Dale & Van Staveren, 2004). Young people, all the while, are becoming more sedentary. Television, computers, and electronic games are often blamed for young teens being less active than their predecessors. But even some school policies contribute to student inactivity. As a way to squeeze more instructional time into the school day, middle schools have cut recess or free time. As a public school student, I walked the seven blocks to and from school each day. Most of my friends did the same or rode a bicycle. Now, the demise of the neighborhood school or safety concerns have resulted in most students being transported to school.

Heredity plays a major role in obesity. Only 10 percent of obese adolescents have parents of normal weight. Having one parent who is obese increases by 40 percent the chances of his or her offspring becoming significantly overweight. If both parents are obese, then adolescent children will be dangerously overweight 70 percent of the time (Santrock, 2005).

Obesity presents immediate problems for an adolescent. Compared to average weight peers, obese teens are absent from school more frequently, and are likely to be depressed and suffer from anxiety disorders (Schwimmer, Burkwinkle, & Varni, 2003). According to the National Diabetes Education Program Web site, Type II diabetes, a malady that used to impact middle aged adults, now impairs the health of overweight teens at an alarming rate. Obese teens also suffer from poor body image, which negatively impacts their self-concept. Our society teaches people at a young age that the endomorphic (plump) body type is not favored in our culture. I recall reading a study several years ago in which preschoolers were shown silhouettes of human figures. They were asked to sort them into two categories—*People you would like to have as your friend* and *People you would not want to be your friend.* Invariably, the portly figures were rejected by five-year-olds as people with whom they would not want to associate.

Not only does being extremely overweight cause immediate problems for adolescents but it likely spells trouble for them as adults. Nearly four in five overweight adolescents will become obese adults (Satcher, 2005). This is a concern because several serious health conditions such as heart disease, stroke, diabetes, joint disorders, gall bladder disease, cancer, and high blood pressure are associated with and complicated by obesity.

Anorexia. Until recently, it was believed anorexia was a disorder that impacted mostly young Caucasian girls from affluent families. But now this potentially fatal disorder is becoming more commonly diagnosed among adolescents of both sexes and all races. Recent reports have identified anorexics as young as nine years old. Middle-aged adults have also been detected with this eating disorder. Anorexia has been diagnosed in 2.5 million Americans, and more people die of this disease than any other mental illness. For those who do fall victim to this malady, the recovery rate is only 50 percent (Tyre, 2005).

Anorexia nervosa is defined as a mental illness in which an individual is obsessed with food and a fear of becoming overweight. Anorexia is generally accompanied by the following characteristics (Santrock, 2005):

- A body weight that is less than 85 percent of what is considered normal for one's age, height, and sex.
- An extreme fear of gaining weight, which persists even with dieting and weight loss.
- A distorted body image; never seeing oneself as "thin enough."

(p. 185)

Due to their obsession with thinness, anorexics may exhibit some extreme behaviors. Obviously, their food intake is generally minimal. But they frequently will exercise to excess in order to burn unwanted calories. They monitor their body mass by weighing themselves frequently and measure their abdomen and thighs regularly. When they look at their image in a mirror, they see "fat" regardless of how thin they have become.

It used to be thought that anorexia was brought on by stress and pressure to be perfect in every way. As youngsters became frustrated with the unrealistic goal of perfection, realizing that not every aspect of their being is within their power to manage, they focused on their body weight as something which they could control. "Doctors now compare anorexia to alcoholism and depression, potentially fatal diseases that may be set off by environmental factors such as stress or trauma, but have their roots in a complex combination of genes and brain chemistry" (Tyre, 2005, pp. 52-53). For individuals who do have a predisposition to develop anorexia, environmental factors and our society's projection of "thinness as beauty" may be among the factors that push vulnerable teens over the edge.

Bulimia. Bulimia nervosa is similar to anorexia in that the afflicted individual is overly concerned about gaining weight and driven by a strong desire to be thin. While the anorexic maintains weight through controlled starvation, most bulimics are unable to restrict their eating habits. Instead, bulimic individuals go through episodes of binge eating followed by a purging of the food, forcing themselves to vomit or using laxatives. It is not unusual for adolescents and young adults to experiment with bulimia. Any signs of bulimic behavior are reason for concern, but it is not considered a serious disorder until an individual binges and purges twice weekly during a three-month period (Santrock, 2005).

While the motivation for bulimia and anorexia are similar, the negative impact of both on the developing human body can be devastating. Reduced amounts of vital nutrients impede normal development. Lack of protein and important minerals in the diet can retard skeletal development and set the stage for conditions such as osteoporosis later in life (Loosli & Ruud, 1998). It is possible for anorexic individuals to lose so much weight that they develop symptoms of starvation including low blood pressure, sensitivity to low temperatures, and constipation. Anorexia is fatal to about 10 percent of its victims, a mortality rate that is 12 times higher than any other cause of death among adolescent and young adult women (Bardick, Dernes, McCulloch, Witko, Spriddle, & Roest, 2004). For bulimics the condition is easier to mask since most bulimics maintain a normal body weight and exhibit normal eating habits between their bouts of bingeing and purging. Bulimia is psychologically harmful because most bulimics recognize their eating habits are not normal and feel guilty about engaging in such behavior. Bulimics often suffer damage to esophagus and teeth by contact with gastric acids regurgitated as a result of frequent purging (Arnett, 2004).

Sleep. One area of young adolescent health frequently ignored is the need for proper rest and sleep. Little research has been conducted on the sleep requirements of young teens and adolescents, but recent findings indicate that teens are among the most sleep-deprived groups in our population (Carskadon, 2002). Parents need to establish house rules and monitor as best they can the sleep of their young teens.

When left to their own devices, adolescents tend to stay up late and "sleep in" the next morning. For years, this observable change in sleep patterns was attributed to external causes such as the need to study more, participation in extracurricular activities, socializing with friends, holding a job, or simply a need to assert their independence (Wolfe, 2005). But more recent research has caused adults to rethink assumptions about the sleep requirements of adolescents. Mary Carskadon (1999), a sleep expert at Brown University, found the sleep requirements of teens were more like children than adults. The prevailing standard has been that young children require a minimum ten hours of sleep per night and that adults need at least eight hours per night. The increased sleep needs for children is attributed to the fact that growth hormones are released during sleep, therefore linking physical growth to sufficient rest (Berger, 2006). Since young adolescents experience a tremendous spurt of physical growth, it is logical that they also require more sleep than previously thought. Carskadon also found that the internal biological clock which regulates the human sleep cycle is different for adolescents as compared to adults and children. Melatonin is a hormone which causes drowsiness and eventually sleep, when released into the bloodstream. Carskadon's research discovered that as teens progress through puberty, melatonin is secreted later at night. The result is that teens tend to stay up later because they do not feel sleepy. But the price is paid on the other end when they are required to "rise and shine" before their sleep cycle has been completed.

The school-related consequences of sleep deprivation are well documented. Students who lack sleep have poorer attendance records, are less motivated, have trouble focusing on tasks, and exhibit more emotional and behavioral problems.

In response to the biologically based sleep requirements, some school systems have moved the start of the school day to later in the morning for middle and high school students. A school district in Minnesota found that shifting their opening bell to a significantly later start time resulted in students being more alert and less depressed while academic achievement improved (Wolfe, 2005). But resolving this issue is not as simple as moving the starting time of middle and high schools back 30 minutes or an hour. The schedules of most middle and high schools are interwoven with elementary schools' timetables and bus routes. Adjusting the schedule has a domino effect. Parents might face child care issues. Co-curricular activities and athletic events would be impacted as well. Wahlstrom (1999) summed up the complexity of this issue by saying, "A school's starting time sets the rhythm for the day for teachers, parents, students, and members of the community at large" (p. 346).

Substance use. The prevalence of harmful substances available to young people is a scary proposition, especially to parents. Young adolescents want to experience new things, fit in with their peers, and ignore the dangers inherent with substance use, all of which make them especially vulnerable to the allures of tobacco, alcohol, and drugs.

Tobacco. Young teens understand that smoking tobacco is hazardous to their health; but still, too many young adolescents take up the habit. Fortunately, there is good news about cigarette use among young teens. Tobacco use is decreasing. Since reaching an all-time high in 1996, smoking rates reported by eighth graders in the U. S. have decreased by 50 percent (Santrock, 2005). In 2005, only 8 percent of eighth-grade students in Vermont reported smoking cigarettes during the previous 30 days, compared to 29 percent in 1995 (Vermont Department of Health, 2005). Increases in the price of cigarettes, more antismoking campaigns coupled with less marketing of tobacco to kids, and less social acceptance of smoking are likely reasons for the decline in teen smoking.

Although tobacco use is on the decline for young adolescents, there remains cause for concern for those who do take up the habit. While people can begin smoking at any age, most smokers try their first cigarette between seventh and ninth grade. For smokers who begin early in life the long-term effects are more severe than for people who wait until they are older. Youngsters who started smoking by age 12 were found to be heavier smokers as adults compared to other smokers who started later in life. Smoking during adolescence has also been linked to permanent pulmonary damage and genetic alterations in the lungs that increase their risk for cancer even if the individual quits smoking in the future. Also, individuals who began smoking as adolescents were found to have a greater risk of developing anxiety disorders and depression as adults (Santrock, 2005).

Alcohol. Though it is illegal in all states for adolescents to drink, a good many do. According to Arnett (2004), alcohol is the most experimental substance of choice by young adolescents. Nearly half (47%) of all eighth graders have tried alcohol, and 21 percent reported they have been intoxicated. These statistics are disturbing since the aftermath of alcohol abuse for individuals is well known. Early drinking increases the chances for an individual to develop alcohol dependency or abuse at some point during his or her life. For adolescents who began drinking before age 18, nearly 17 percent were later classified as alcohol dependent while 7.8 percent were diagnosed with alcohol abuse. In 2001, three million adolescents from ages 12 to 20 had developed significant drinking problems and were classified

Nearly half of all eighth graders have tried alcohol, and 21 percent reported they have been intoxicated.

as "alcohol dependent" (U.S. Department of Health and Human Services, 2003). For persons who waited until age 21 to take their first drink, the risk of developing alcohol dependency and abuse dropped by over 60 percent. So the well-documented dangers associated with long-term drinking markedly increase for individuals who begin drinking as young adolescents.

Recent research indicates that alcohol affects teens and adults differently. These findings signal new reasons for alarm when adolescents consume alcohol. As was reported in Chapter 1, the young adolescent brain is still maturing and under construction. The frontal cortex, which is responsible for processing information, and the hippocampus, which is associated with learning and memory, are still developing. The Society for Neuroscience (2002) reported experiments conducted on rats that were of comparable maturity to human teens revealed that alcohol consumed by young rodents impaired their ability to perform learning and memory tasks. Also, the impact of the alcohol had a more damaging effect on the brains of adolescent rats than it did on the adult control group. Obviously, the ethical issues of providing alcohol to underage teens prevents such experiments being replicated on human subjects. But the logical findings imply that alcohol consumption during adolescence has a more devastating effect on brain development and function than for adults.

While teens are likely more vulnerable to neurological impairment due to the influence of alcohol compared to adults, evidence exists which indicates that young teens are less sensitive than adults to other effects of alcohol use. White (2004) reported tests performed on laboratory rats revealed that adolescent rodents were less sensitive to the sedation effects of alcohol compared to adult rats. The same finding was true when the effect on motor skills was tested. So while adult rats became listless and drowsy and lost muscle coordination when exposed to intoxicating doses of alcohol, their adolescent counterparts remained alert and in normal control of body movements while under the influence of alcohol. Since the experiments were performed on rodents, it is difficult to say with certainty that the same results hold true for humans. But the neurobiology of rats is similar to humans. Therefore, it is logical to conclude that the research findings on adult and adolescent differences in how rats respond to alcohol would apply to humans as well (White, 2004).

The tendency for teen drinkers to remain alert and coordinated while under the influence is unfortunate. When adults have had too much to drink, they may become so incapacitated that they cannot continue to over-indulge, while teens may continue to drink when intoxicated by giving a false sense of sobriety. This could be one reason why young teens are prone to binge drinking—the consumption of five or more alcoholic drinks within a couple of hours. Since the teen feels in control of her body and is wide awake, she may continue to drink large quantities of alcohol in one sitting. Seven percent of Vermont eighth-grade students reported they had participated in binge drinking (Vermont Department of Health, 2005). Such behavior can be fatal due to alcohol poisoning.

Altogether there is sufficient evidence to show that alcohol consumption by young adolescents represents a real threat to their cognitive development and future well-being.

Drugs. Where does one begin? We now live in a drug-saturated society. While the nicotine contained in tobacco and the alcohol in beverages are drugs, the word usually conjures up images of illegal substances peddled on street corners by the underworld. Frequently, we hear of new recreational drugs that just hit the streets, and teens are often portrayed as eager to try any new substance that will give them a buzz. But Arnett (2004) assured us that drug use among American teens is not as rampant as our perceptions may lead us to believe. After surveying high school seniors, Arnett found that only 17 percent had ever tried amphetamines, 12 percent had experimented with inhalants, 11 percent had sampled ecstasy, and 8 percent had used cocaine. Frequent use of these substances was rarely reported. Even so those adolescents who struggle with drug use do face serious potential for addiction and associated health hazards. The sections that follow will focus on those substances most frequently encountered by young adolescents.

> Drug use among American teens is not as rampant as our perceptions may lead us to believe.

Prescription drugs—tranquilizers, pain killers, stimulants, and sedatives—are currently among the substances most abused by young people in the United States. Young teens often experiment with these easy-to-obtain drugs to see what effect they will have on their bodies. Seldom are they aware of the health risks involved or the addictive nature of some medications that make these drugs especially dangerous. Home medicine cabinets are a frequent source of such drugs. These drugs also are pilfered from school infirmaries or from people for whom the medication was ordered (National Drug Intelligence Center, 2002). Middle schools have initiated strict policies about the possession and use of prescription and even over-the-counter drugs. In schools, all drugs are expected to be secured in the school infirmary and kept in the original container.

Inhalants, as the name implies, are substances that emit fumes intentionally inhaled by individuals in order to "get high." Fumes from products such as gasoline, paint, glue, correction fluid, cleaning agents, aerosol containers, and felt tipped markers are sniffed directly from the container, from a bag in which the substance was placed, or from a cloth soaked in the substance. Inhalants are popular among young adolescents because they are legal, easily obtained, and found in abundant supply in most homes and schools. The use of inhalants is also difficult to detect by others. Young adolescents do not grasp the consequences of abusing the fumes from products found under the kitchen sink or in the school's art room supply closet, but the gases from inhalants can damage the brain, liver, kidneys, and sense of hearing. Death can even occur for first time users. High concentrations of inhalants can cause suffocation because the gases displace oxygen in the lungs and impact the central nervous system, causing breathing to cease. Chemicals in solvents and aerosol containers have been known to cause death due to heart failure (Focus Adolescent Services, 2000).

Marijuana is a hallucinogen derived from a hemp plant commonly grown in many parts of the world. It is the most heavily used drug among young teens but its use has been on a decline in recent years after spiking in the mid-1990s. Sixteen percent of eighth graders in Vermont reported having at least tried marijuana and 8 percent said they tried the drug before age 13 (Vermont Department of Health, 2005). While fewer teens are using marijuana, the bad news is that the potency of the drug has increased about fivefold in recent years (Preboth, 2000), making it more toxic for even casual users.

Marijuana impacts the user in several ways. The physical effects of marijuana on the body include dry mouth, irritation and reddening of the eyes, coughing, escalated pulse rate, and elevated blood pressure. Marijuana use can cause individuals to form disjointed ideas, become disoriented, and become more sensitive to auditory and visual stimulation. The academic life of marijuana users is compromised because the drug has a negative impact on memory and the ability to focus attention. Long term and heavy marijuana use can also affect fertility and may be associated with specific birth defects (Santock, 2005).

Sequence of substance use

Research has shown that teens who use substances do so in a highly predictable sequence (Kandel, 1975):

1. Drinking beer and wine
2. Smoking cigarettes and drinking hard liquor
3. Smoking marijuana
4. Using hard drugs such as LSD or cocaine (p. 913)

Since Kandel's work 30 years ago, cigarettes, beer, and wine have been referred to as "gateway drugs." By examining the sequence above, one might erroneously assume that once a youngster samples his first drink of beer or wine, he is on a slippery slope that will ultimately lead to hard-core drug use. Kandel (2002) clarified the gateway hypothesis by emphasizing that youngsters who use hard drugs have invariably passed through the gates of alcohol, cigarettes, and marijuana use. Hardly ever does a teen who experiments with illicit substances begin with hard drugs. Nor does drinking beer or wine seal one's fate that she will eventually progress to the next level. The gateway drug theory suggests that teens at a given level on the continuum have previously tried the substances at the lower levels (i.e. marijuana users have nearly always used cigarettes and alcohol), but it does not mean that youngsters are more likely to move to the next stage of involvement compared to teens who have not engaged in substance use at all. It is incorrect to conclude that experimentation with gateway drugs will necessarily cause an individual to later use more potent substances (Arnett, 2004).

Emotional issues

Not all ailments that impact young adolescents affect their physical health. Young adolescents frequently deal with situations and circumstances that tax their mental health as well. Many of these conditions may impact the emotional and psychological status of middle level students. Some of the most common disorders that cause emotional turmoil are outlined in the following sections.

Stress. In a survey of more than 700 young adolescents, 20 percent of them reported that they were experiencing stressful circumstances and needed help to cope with the situation (Hayes & Morgan, 2005). If young adolescents are observed for any length of time, one could easily conclude that their entire existence consists of a never-ending litany of one crisis after another. From an adult perspective, many of the issues over which young adolescents "stress out" are trivial in the grand scheme of things. Yet, to the young adolescent, the stress is real. Going through the physical changes of puberty, dealing with feelings and emotions they have never experienced before, coping with peer expectations, and making the transition from elementary to middle school can be stressful for almost all young adolescents.

According to Ebata (1994), adolescents react to stress in much the same ways as adults by showing signs of fear, anxiety, sadness, and anger. While each adolescent will respond in unique ways, stress usually produces a change in one's pattern of behavior. Some youngsters will withdraw, others will lash out, and some will confide in others for support. After studying adolescents coping with stress, Ebata found that an accumulation of stressful events during a short period of time is more difficult for young adolescents to handle than a single event; and sustained, routine stressors are more difficult to withstand than major life events that alter the day-to-day routines of young adolescents.

When adolescents were studied to determine what specific problems produced stress for them, the issues identified focused around a sense of loss or conflict. Specifically, teens reported increased stress when they experienced loss through a break-up of a romantic relationship, change in financial status of the family, or illness or injury of a family member. Arguments with parents, trouble with siblings, witnessing arguments between parents, and clashes with peers were other common conflicts young teens reported as stressors (Walker, 2002).

CASE STUDY

STRESSED OUT AND OVER-SCHEDULED AT AGE 13?

Jackie is a good student and has always done well in school. But now that she's in middle school, her parents are adamant that she earn top marks in every class since grades now "count." Jackie is active in several cocurricular activities that interest her. But her parents insist she be involved in enrichment activities and community events, which they think will look good on her resumé. Jackie and her classmates are constantly reminded by their teachers of the importance of doing well on standardized tests so the school can demonstrate it is making Adequate Yearly Progress. The end result is that Jackie is overscheduled and stressed out because of the demands placed on her time and energy. Jackie comes to you, one of her teachers, for advice. What do you suggest?

1. Encourage her to speak with her guidance counselor.
2. Tell her to get used to the demands of being an adolescent approaching maturity.
3. Speak to her parents about the demands on their daughter.
4. Talk with Jackie about this issue and work with her and her parents to set a realistic schedule that will alleviate the stress she feels.
5. Other _____

Comment:

Schools can be a major stressor for young adolescents. In today's climate of academic accountability, competition, and achievement, students at all levels feel the pressure to excel and perform. The perceived need to take rigorous courses, achieve high marks in class, and pack one's resumé with worthwhile activities impacts middle level students. Schools are beginning to recognize that the push for academic achievement may be counterproductive to overall learning and even detrimental to the health of students.

Many schools are beginning to take steps to change our culture's paradigm of success and achievement. Even high-status institutions such as Stanford University and Massachusetts Institute of Technology have made changes in their admission policies emphasizing that young students do not have to be "super teens" to get attention from elite institutions. MIT now places a limit on the number of cocurricular activities one can list on resumés. Stanford asks its applicants to write an essay about what they find exciting and motivating. Stanford also explains that they do not necessarily accept students who have taken the most advanced placement courses (Pope & Simon, 2005). Policies such as these should send messages to young students, and adults who work with them, that one need not perform Herculean feats in multiple arenas to excel in future endeavors.

Depression. Since young teens tend to be moody, serious depression can easily be overlooked or dismissed by parents or teachers as a normal, though irritating, symptom of adolescence. However, depression can lead to severe emotional disturbances and even to self-destructive behavior; the symptoms of depression should not be ignored. According to the National Mental Health Association (2006), signs of adolescent depression include poor school performance, withdrawal from friends and activities, extreme sadness, sense of hopelessness, loss of enthusiasm or motivation, low energy level, anger or rage, overreaction to criticism, changes in eating and sleeping patterns, and inability to concentrate. These symptoms are especially worrisome if they persist for longer than two weeks.

Depression is a fairly common disorder among adolescents. It is estimated that 15 to 20 percent of teens will experience depression during their adolescent years. Teens who exhibit at least two risk factors, such as insecure attachment to parents, an anxious temperament, minimal coping skills, or early onset of puberty are more prone to depression. Girls usually outnumber boys diagnosed with depression by a two-to-one ratio. (Petersen & Stemmler, 2005). While the reasons why girls are twice as likely as boys to experience depression are not completely clear, biological differences and cultural expectations that impact boys and girls appear to account for the variance. Also, young adolescents who are regularly left home alone unsupervised for longer than three hours a day are more likely to become depressed (Mertens, Flowers, & Mulhall, 2003). It also is common for individuals who suffer from depression to have a family history of emotional disorders (Schlozman, 2001).

Not only is depression debilitating for youth so afflicted, the link to adolescent suicide is frightening. Major depression has been identified as a predictive indicator of suicidal thoughts and attempts for both male and female adolescents (Kelly, Lynch, Donovan, & Clark, 2001). For this reason, symptoms of adolescent depression should not be ignored, and professional help should possibly be sought.

Helping young adolescents cope with stress

Young adolescents need adults who are their advocates. Obviously parents—but also middle level teachers—most naturally fill this advocacy role. Ebata (1994) offered three major ways and specific examples of how caring adults can help young adolescents deal with stressful situations.

1. Provide help, encouragement, and support.
   - Encourage teens to talk about their problems.
   - Listen to their concerns.
   - Do not offer advice unless it is requested.
   - Do not minimize or trivialize their concern.
   - Offer reassurance, encouragement, and support.
   - Continue to provide structure and stability by holding fast to rules, procedures, and routines.

2. Help young teens develop coping skills.
   - Model effective coping skills and talk about how you deal with stress.
   - Help teens develop multiple ways to cope with difficulties and to evaluate the pros and cons of each.
   - Help them find safe ways to "blow off steam" and relax.
   - Help them seek the positive side of problems by looking at situations from multiple perspectives.

3. Take care of yourself.
   - Pay attention to your own stress level and act to reduce your own stress.
   - Seek help and support from others by talking with a trusted friend or professional if you feel overwhelmed. (pp. 2–3)

Adolescent sexuality and health

A few years ago I attended a workshop for parents of young adolescents that focused on the sexual behavior of middle school students. The facilitator began by asking rhetorically how many parents thought their child was sexually active. I remember gasps and heads shaking in denial when she went on to state with confidence that nearly all of their children were sexually active. The parents were conditioned to think, like most of our culture, that being sexually active equated to engaging in full intercourse. Her point was that the sexual awakening that nearly all young adolescents experience is a normal and natural part of growing up.

Although most young teens do not act on their sexual feelings by engaging in sexual intercourse, they do spend considerable time trying to figure out this new dimension of self.

While sexual intercourse is a highly researched aspect of teen sexual behavior, youngsters have many innocent sexual experiences that proceed, in most cases, sexual intercourse by several years. From this viewpoint, youngsters who engage in flirting behavior or holding hands are sexually active. According to Brooks-Gunn and Paikoff (1993) teen sexual behavior generally progresses through several stages that usually last several years. Masturbation is generally the first step in the progression, followed by kissing, then necking and petting, sexual intercourse, and finally oral sex. However, a recent study from the University of California (2005) indicated that young adolescents engage in oral sex at a higher rate than vaginal sex. Nearly one in five (19.6%) of the ninth graders surveyed reported that they had tried oral sex compared to 13.5 percent who said they had tried vaginal intercourse. The young teens who engaged in oral sex said they believed the practice was safer for their physical and emotional health and was more acceptable among their peers. Adults who counsel teens need to be aware of these attitudes as they become prevalent among young adolescents.

One should not believe that all teens complete the progression outlined above. While teens are often viewed as promiscuous, the percentage of adolescents who reported having sex has declined over the last several years. The Centers for Disease Control (2002) found that the percentage of teens who reported ever having had sexual intercourse decreased from 54.1 percent in 1991 to 45.6 percent in 2001. While this downward trend for all teens appears promising, Manlove and Terry (2000) found that the proportion of girls age 14 and younger who experienced their first sexual intercourse had increased significantly over the last decade. This indicates that the total number of teens having sex may be declining, but those who do engage in sex are doing so at a younger age.

There are many reasons why delaying sexual involvement until adulthood is a good idea. Young adolescents who are biologically ready for sexual activity are almost never prepared to deal with the complex emotional issues of such experiences at this age. These research findings highlight some of the negative issues associated with early sexual intercourse for young adolescents (Brown & Flanigan, 2003):

- Early sexual experience is linked to having multiple sexual partners over time, increasing one's risk of teen pregnancy and exposure to sexually transmitted diseases.
- The younger a female was at the time of her first sexual experience, the more likely that the episode was unwanted.

136

- Over 80 percent of sexually active young adolescents reported that they wished they had postponed sex until they were older.
- Girls who give birth at age 14 or younger are at high risk for having children born with health problems. About one in seven girls who engaged in sexual intercourse by age 14 became pregnant.
- Young adolescents who become parents almost never have the resources or parenting skills to care for an infant without substantial help and support from older relatives or friends. Unwanted teen pregnancy may not really be just a teen problem since 60 percent of teen births are fathered by adult males.
- Sexual intercourse between young adolescents frequently puts young teens in conflict with "age of consent" laws, which are set at age 16 in over half of the states in this country. (pp. 6–7)

Dissuading young adolescents from engaging in sexual activity is clearly a sound position. Discouraging early dating especially with a significantly older partner, monitoring and supervising social activities, communicating with young teens about sexual behavior and expectations, and providing factual and accurate information at an early age are important steps parents and adults can take to help young teens postpone sex.

American young adolescents live in a culture that is steeped in sexuality and our society sends many confusing messages to our youth about sexual behavior. The media are saturated with sexually suggestive and even graphic images. The constant bombardment of sexual messages on young adolescents may lead to cavalier attitudes about sex and lead to irresponsible and dangerous behavior. The glamorous portrayal of sex by the media needs to be balanced by open, frank, and factual discussions about the likely consequences of early sexual activity.

Sexually transmitted diseases

Aside from the risk of unwanted pregnancy and the emotional trauma that can result from early sexual experimentation, young adolescents put their health in jeopardy when engaging in sexual behavior. Several dangerous diseases lurk for those individuals who put themselves in compromising situations. Sexually transmitted diseases (STDs) are infections caused by viruses or bacteria being passed from one individual to another by sexual contact. Young adolescents are especially vulnerable to the damaging effects of sexually transmitted infections because they are generally reluctant to seek treatment and may not tell their partner about their suspected condition (Berger, 2006).

Chlamydia, gonorrhea, genital herpes, syphilis, and HIV/AIDS are sexually transmitted diseases to which young adolescents are frequently exposed. Chlamydia (the most commonly diagnosed STD among adolescents), gonorrhea, and syphilis are caused by bacteria. Frequently these infections produce few, if any, symptoms initially. But left untreated these diseases can harm internal organs and cause permanent infertility. Because gonorrhea, syphilis, and chlamydia are caused by bacteria, these infections do respond well to treatment by antibiotics. Genital herpes and HIV/AIDS infections, on the other hand, are extremely difficult to treat since they are caused by viruses and are resistant to drug therapy. Genital herpes, referred to as herpes simplex II (HSV-2), is highly contagious and produces sores or blisters on the genitals that persist for as long as six weeks. The virus is spread through close personal contact while the infected partner has an active lesion. While other STDs have been around for centuries, HIV/AIDS is a newcomer first diagnosed in 1981. The devastating effect this disease has on the body is well documented. The AIDS virus disables the body's immune system and renders it helpless to ward off other diseases and infections. The virus responsible for AIDS is found in body fluids of infected individuals. So any circumstance that puts one in contact with blood, semen, or vaginal secretions of infected persons puts an individual at risk for contracting AIDS (Arnett, 2004).

Because the microbes which cause STDs thrive in a warm, moist environment, the internal structure of the female genitalia makes it an ideal incubator for bacteria and viruses to grow. For this reason, females are more prone to contract STDs than males. This difference in anatomy at least partially explains why girls are twice as likely as boys to contract chlamydia or gonorrhea following even one episode of unprotected sex (Encyclopedia of Children's Health, http://health.enotes.com/childrens-health-encyclopedia/). Obviously, abstention from sexual activity is the only sure method to prevent contracting most STDs. But limiting the number of sex partners, having a mutually monogamous relationship, and using condoms during each sex act are known to reduce the risk of being infected.

Sexuality education

No group is more interested in the sexual development and behavior of young teens than young adolescents themselves. As in all other aspects of their development, 10- to 15-year-olds need and deserve accurate information about their burgeoning sexuality. Parents should be the major source of information about sexuality for a variety of reasons. Parents know their child best and should have an idea how their child will respond to discussing sexual themes, allowing them the luxury of choosing the right time and place for delicate discussions. Sexual attitudes and behaviors involve moral issues, and parents are the best source to convey family values concerning such issues. Be that as it may, many parents disregard their obligation to educate their children about sexual matters, leaving the bulk of the responsibility to the schools.

Middle schools have a responsibility to provide young teens with factual information to help them understand their sexual development and make responsible decisions about their behavior. The problem for schools is to devise a sex education curriculum that is broad enough in scope to meet the needs of all young adolescents. I remember one year having students who were still interested in Barbie dolls and GI Joes and a 13-year-old classmate who had given birth. Considering the huge range of maturity and experience of middle level students, developing a relevant curriculum is an imposing task. Yet, most adults believe that schools should be involved in sex education and employ what is known as an abstinence-plus sex education program. Such curricula teach that the only sure way to protect oneself from pregnancy and sexually transmitted diseases is to refrain from sexual activity. But such programs recognize that "just say no" will not be effective for all teens and inform youngsters about condom use and other effective measures to guard their health and well-being. Not all school districts have a system wide sex education program, but for those that do, two-thirds endorse the abstinence-plus approach (Kirby, 2000).

Leading causes of death among adolescents

Nothing is more heartbreaking than burying a child. I frequently tell my preservice teachers that during their careers they will likely have to help their students work through the trauma caused by the death of a classmate. Young people just getting a foothold on life are not supposed to die. When the major reasons for adolescent death in the United States are examined, we can readily conclude that most adolescent deaths could be prevented, since most adolescent mortality is attributed to teen behavior rather than catastrophic illnesses. Accidents, homicide, and suicide are the three leading causes of death among teenagers in the United States (U.S. National Library of Medicine, 2005).

Adolescent death and accidents. Accidents claim the lives of more young teens than any other factor. Motor vehicle accidents by far are the most common cause of fatalities among teens. While most middle school students are too young to legally drive a car, they are frequently passengers in vehicles operated by inexperienced drivers. According to the Vermont Youth Risk Behavior Survey (Vermont Department of Health, 2005), 34 percent of eighth graders surveyed revealed that they had been injured in an automobile crash with a 17-year-old or younger driver; and 41 percent of those students reported not wearing a seat belt at the time of the crash. The small town where I live was stunned recently by such a tragedy. On a snowy highway, a 16-year-old driver slid into the path of an oncoming school bus. The driver of the car was killed and her 14-year-old unbelted passenger was thrown from the car and received fatal injuries.

Possessing keen senses and quick reflexes, teen drivers are physically equipped to be the best drivers on the road. But their lack of experience behind the wheel and lapses in judgment place them at a high risk for causing accidents. Not using seat belts is another practice that has the potential to turn an accident into a tragedy. Put alcohol into the equation, as it often is, and the potential for somber newspaper headlines increases markedly. Unintentional gunshot wounds, drowning, and burns resulting from fires are other leading causes of accidental deaths among teens.

Adolescent death and homicide. If an accidental death of a young person seems tragic, imagine the loss of a young life due to murder. Gang violence and crime in urban areas account for many violent deaths among young people in the United States. African American males are three times more likely to die of a homicide than they are to die from natural causes (Santrock, 2005). The easy access to guns in our country is likely a factor why so many disputes between angry individuals are settled with a firearm.

Obviously not every adolescent murder is a result of urban crime. The stream of school shootings in small towns and suburban areas of our country over the last decade and the April 2007 tragedy at Virginia Tech increase cause for deep concern. The perpetrators of several fatal school shootings in rural areas possessed six of the common risk factors—peer rejection, threatening others verbally, interest in violent media, suicidal thoughts, previous violent behavior, and violent writing (Kidd & Meyer, 2002). The middle school ideal of having every student known well by at least one caring adult in the school could go a long way to reach out to neglected and rejected students who might be prone to extreme violence.

Adolescent death and suicide. It is hard to imagine young people being so desperate and hopeless that they contemplate, and even act on, ending their own lives. Adolescents tend to be impulsive. They sometimes view a temporary situation as a permanent condition, which may cause them to respond in a self-destructive manner (National Mental Health Association, 2006). Sadly, suicide is the third leading cause of death among adolescents in this country. Studies reveal nearly 20 percent of adolescents have thought about committing suicide at some point in their lives. But, fortunately, of those who have contemplated suicide only a small portion, less than 2 percent, act on their thoughts. Girls have a much higher rate of suicide attempts compared to boys but males are more successful in complet-

Suicide is the third leading cause of death among adolescents in this country.

ing the act because they tend to use more lethal and immediate means to end their own lives (Santrock, 2005). For students 10 to 14, the number of suicides increased 100 percent between 1980 and 1996. No child should suffer an emotional crisis that could cause her to take her own life. Because poor mental health impedes academic achievement, educators are obligated to do everything they can to promote good mental health among their students. Yet, for a variety of reasons, ranging from liability to confidentiality, schools generally find it difficult to identify their proper role in preventing suicide in young teens (Franklin, 2005b).

Any premature death is tragic, but when the death is caused by a youngster's own hand the aftermath is even more devastating. People close to the deceased are left to question "why" and wonder what they could have done to prevent the tragedy. While suicidal behavior is difficult, or even impossible, to predict, some indicators of potential suicides have been identified. Extreme and chronic stress has been found to precede suicide attempts in males while low self-esteem and family dysfunction were identified predictors of suicidal behavior in female adolescents. Depression has been found to be a major factor in adolescent suicide for both genders (Kelly, Lynch, Donovan, & Clark, 2001). Youngsters who have experienced abuse are more likely to exhibit a tendency toward suicide (Evans, Hawton, & Rodham, 2005). Genetics also seems to play a role in those prone to suicide. If a youngster has a close blood relative who has committed suicide, that factor raises the probability of the teen replicating the act (Santrock, 2005). There is also a tendency for adolescent suicides to occur in clusters, sometimes referred to as "copycat" events. This phenomenon questions the amount of exposure that should be given to youth suicides. Studies indicate that suicide attempts increase proportionately to the level of media coverage devoted to an adolescent who ends his own life (Becker & Schmidt, 2005). This same copycat possibility should be strongly considered when schools counsel young adolescents who have lost a peer or family member to suicide.

Warning signs

Eighty percent of adolescents who attempt suicide give clear warning signs prior to their attempt. In addition to the signals given in the case study above, other warning signs include (National Mental Health Association, 2006):

- Direct or indirect suicidal threats.
- Obsession with death.
- Irrational or bizarre behavior.
- Extreme sense of guilt, shame, or rejection.
- Major changes in eating or sleeping habits.
- Giving away of possessions.

It is important to take the warning signs of suicide seriously. Trust your instincts. If you believe a young teen is in trouble, he probably is! A youngster who has made a plan or expressed a specific method for ending his or her life is of special concern. Do not leave such youngsters alone, and get professional help immediately.

ARE THERE WARNING SIGNS?

Jessica, an eighth grader, has been a member of Ms. Clark's teacher advisory group for two years. Jessica is a good student, has many friends, is generally happy and pleasant, and comes to school neatly dressed and well groomed. But over the last several weeks, Ms. Clark has observed that Jessica's mood has been more somber. With her grades declining, she frequently comes to school looking a bit disheveled, and Jessica has withdrawn from her peers. Ms. Clark recently found a poem Jessica had written that contained many references to the death of young teens. All of these behaviors are recent and a radical departure from Jessica's typical behavior. Ms. Clark is worried about Jessica. What should she do?

1. Speak to Jessica about her concerns.
2. Call Jessica's parents and inform them of her observations.
3. Have a knowledgeable school counselor speak to Jessica immediately.
4. Do nothing but continue to observe Jessica's behavior.
5. Other _____

Comment:

All of these behaviors are warning signs of suicidal behavior. While not every young adolescent who exhibits such behavior is ready to end her life, such symptoms should not be ignored. Middle level teachers and advisors are expected to be advocates for their students, but many educators do not feel comfortable or have the necessary expertise to deal with serious mental health issues. Teacher advisors and classroom teachers are not expected to help students unravel such complex issues. But at the very least, Ms. Clark should inform the school counselor immediately with her concerns and follow through to make sure a qualified professional begins to address Jessica's behavior and its underlying causes.

In summary

Educators at all levels agree there is a clear link between academic performance and the health and well-being of students. Youngsters who are frequently absent from school due to chronic illness or are distracted because of physiological distress simply do not perform to their potential. To advance the intellectual development of its students, good middle schools working with families and community agencies do all they can to promote the health and safety of young people, recognizing health promotion as a part of their mission. ▪

As some young adolescents see it ...

We are smarter than you think we are about serious issues.
Sarah, age 14

*I try to make good choices. I am not stupid and am wise enough
to stay away from things that can hurt me.*
Bobby, age 13

*When adults tell me I can't do something because it isn't safe,
I usually think they are overreacting.
But sometimes, usually later, I see that they were right.*
Adrianna, age 14

9.
Positive Interventions

Growing up has always been a challenging adventure. Today's young people face a multitude of issues, any one of which has the potential to create long-term or permanent havoc for their health and well-being. Some teens emerge from adolescence fully prepared for adulthood, despite having received little guidance or direction from caring adults. Other adolescents, even though supplied with numerous advantages and unlimited support, find themselves shipwrecked because of poor personal decisions. Fortunately, most young adolescents traverse the normal challenges of the age span, just as they should. But many teens who are left adrift to navigate adolescence alone will encounter turbulent times, which have far-reaching effects. This chapter will explore some concepts, principles, and programs that can help young teens make good decisions and enjoy a safe and productive adolescence.

Resiliency

Josh and I grew up in the same small town in the Midwest. He was born into poverty to alcoholic parents who provided little tangible support. Despite having negligible help or encouragement at home, Josh did well in school, had several friends, was involved in extracurricular activities, attended a local church, was active in the youth group, and was a model citizen. He graduated from high school and worked his way through college. Now a middle-aged adult, Josh is a successful businessman and civic leader in a small town near where he was raised. Years ago, Josh would have been referred to as a "self-made man." Today, Josh is considered a resilient individual.

Why was Josh successful in overcoming adversity to become a productive and successful adult when the cards were stacked against him as a youth? Resiliency has been defined as the "ability to develop coping strategies despite adverse conditions, positive responses to negative circumstances, and a protective shield from continuous stressful surroundings" (Brodkin & Coleman, 1996, p. 28). Researchers have studied individuals such as Josh to determine traits they possess that allow them to develop positively in the face of adversity (Wolin & Wolin, 1993). The key characteristics are

- Insight
- Independence
- Relationships
- Initiative
- Creativity
- Humor
- Morality. (p. 248)

By examining this list, it appears that some traits are possessed or developed inherently. Others have to be supplied or nurtured by the family or other sources in the community. Anything that educators and parents can do to foster these traits will go a long way toward helping youngsters survive and thrive whatever their life's circumstances. National Middle School Association (2003) identified specific traits that should be evident in the culture of successful middle schools:

- Educators who desire to work with young adolescents and are specially prepared to do so.
- Courageous and collaborative leadership.
- A shared vision that guides all decisions.
- An inviting, supportive, and safe environment.
- High expectations for all.
- Students and teachers engaged in active learning.
- An adult advocate for every student.
- School-initiated family and community partnerships. (p. 7)

These characteristics of a positive school culture can, directly or indirectly, help all young adolescents build their capacity for resiliency. When we think of creating a supportive school climate, it is assumed that task falls on the shoulders of the certified professionals within the school. But Purkey and Novak (1996) maintain that all non-certified staff play important roles in creating an inviting school environment as well. They suggested specific ways that everyone from cooks to custodians and even bus drivers can help create an affirming school climate. There is much work to do in this area since, according to Scales (1999), only 24 percent of sixth through eighth graders report experiencing a positive school climate, a disturbing finding. While all students benefit from attending schools characterized by such traits, those young adolescents who face adversity or are raised in deprived situations stand to gain the most.

Developmental assets

Raising a young adolescent is a complex proposition. The old African proverb, "It takes a whole village to raise a child," is sound. No one individual, entity, or institution holds the key to helping young adolescents become productive citizens. Search Institute identified 40 positive influences on young adolescents that help them make wise decisions and healthy choices. These 40 positive influences are called *developmental assets* (Benson, 1997). The focus of asset building for adolescents is not only to counter negative outcomes but to "help young people become adults who are healthy, caring, productive, and happy" (Scales, 1996, p. 30).

The Search Institute has separated the 40 developmental resources into *internal assets,* those that individual students must generate for themselves, and *external assets,* which must be supplied from outside sources. Four categories of assets have been identified for both internal and external assets as follows:

External: Support, empowerment, boundaries and expectations, constructive use of time

Internal: Educational commitment, values, social competencies, positive identity

Figure 1 (pp. 148–149) lists these 40 developmental assets under the eight categories. Assets middle schools can most directly affect are italicized.

Middle schools should be major players in helping young adolescents cultivate the desired developmental assets. More than half (22 of 40) of the assets identified fall directly in the province of the middle school, and most others can be indirectly supported by developmentally responsive middle schools. Parents, extended family members, youth organizations, civic groups, and religious denominations all should play roles in helping young adolescents cultivate these assets that fall outside the influence of the school yet will keep them healthy and safe through adolescence and set them on a positive course toward adulthood.

The prevalence of developmental assets

The manner in which developmental assets impact adolescents is straightforward. The more assets a youngster has, the better equipped he or she is to make good choices and flourish. The converse is also true. The Search Institute (1997) established 31 of 40 as the minimum number of assets it hoped adolescents would experience during their middle and high school years. Only about 8 percent of teens surveyed enjoyed that level of support, while 20 percent said they experienced between zero and ten assets. The number of assets reported by teens declined every year from sixth grade through high school, and male adolescents consistently reported fewer assets than their female peers. These figures are a cause for real concern by parents and educators.

FIGURE 1

THE 40 DEVELOPMENTAL ASSETS FOR ADOLESCENTS®

External Assets

Support

1. **Family support**—Family life provides high levels of love and support.
2. **Positive family communication**—Young person and her or his parent(s) communicate positively, and young person is willing to seek advice and counsel from parents.
3. **Other adult relationships**—*Young person receives support from three or more nonparent adults.*
4. **Caring neighborhood**—Young person experiences caring neighbors.
5. **Caring school climate**—*School provides a caring, encouraging environment.*
6. **Parent involvement in schooling**—Parent(s) are actively involved in helping young person succeed in school.

Boundaries and Expectations

11. **Family boundaries**—Family has clear rules and consequences and monitors the young person's whereabouts.
12. **School boundaries**—*School provides clear rules and consequences.*
13. **Neighborhood boundaries**—Neighbors take responsibility for monitoring young people's behavior.
14. **Adult role models**—Parent(s) and other adults model positive, responsible behavior.
15. **Positive peer influence**—Young person's best friends model responsible behavior.
16. **High expectations**—*Both parent(s) and teachers encourage the young person to do well.*

Empowerment

7. **Community values youth**—Young person perceives that adults in the community value youth.
8. **Youth as resources**—Young people are given useful roles in the community.
9. **Service to others**—*Young person serves in the community one hour or more per week.*
10. **Safety**—*Young person feels safe at home, school, and in the neighborhood.*

Constructive Use of Time

17. **Creative activities**—*Young person spends three or more hours per week in lessons or practice in music, theater, or other arts.*
18. **Youth programs**—*Young person spends three or more hours per week in sports, clubs, or organizations at school and/or in the community.*
19. **Religious community**—Young person spends one or more hours per week in activities in a religious institution.
20. **Time at home**—Young person is out with friends "with nothing special to do" two or fewer nights per week.

Internal Assets

Commitment to Learning

21. Achievement motivation—*Young person is motivated to do well in school.*
22. School engagement—*Young person is actively engaged in learning.*
23. Homework—*Young person reports doing at least one hour of homework every school day.*
24. Bonding to school—*Young person cares about her or his school.*
25. Reading for pleasure—*Young person reads for pleasure three or more hours per week.*

Positive Values

26. Caring—*Young person places high value on helping other people.*
27. Equality and social justice—Young person places high value on promoting equality and reducing hunger and poverty.
28. Integrity—Young person acts on convictions and stands up for her or his beliefs.
29. Honesty—*Young person "tells the truth even when it is not easy."*
30. Responsibility—*Young person accepts and takes personal responsibility.*
31. Restraint—*Young person believes it is important not to be sexually active or to use alcohol or other drugs.*

Social Competencies

32. Planning and decision making—*Young person knows how to plan ahead and make choices.*
33. Interpersonal competence—Young person has empathy, sensitivity, and friendship skills.
34. Cultural competence—*Young person has knowledge of and comfort with people of different cultural/racial/ethnic backgrounds.*
35. Resistance skills—*Young person can resist negative peer pressure and dangerous situations.*
36. Peaceful conflict resolution—*Young person seeks to resolve conflict nonviolently.*

Positive Identity

37. Personal power—*Young person feels he or she has control over "things that happen to me."*
38. Self-esteem—Young person reports having a high self-esteem.
39. Sense of purpose—Young person reports that "my life has a purpose."
40. Positive view of personal future—Young person is optimistic about her or his personal future.

In 1997 the 40 developmental assets developed by the Search Institute were used to survey middle and high school students in Vermont to assess their health and well-being. The survey revealed that adolescents' behavior was directly related to the number of assets they had. According to the Vermont survey, adolescents who had 31 to 40 assets demonstrated six *thriving indicators*. (Thriving indicators included behaviors such as school success, informal helping, valuing diversity, maintaining good health, exhibiting leadership, resisting danger, impulse control, and overcoming adversity). If one would envision a young adolescent characterized by any six of the thriving indicators listed above, one would have a prototype for a youngster who "had her act together." Students who reported zero to 10 assets averaged less than three thriving indicators, making for a less productive youngster. Not surprisingly, the results showed that the more developmental assets adolescents experienced, the more thriving behaviors were evident in their lives (Vermont Agency of Human Services, 1998).

The power of assets to shield youngsters from risky or unhealthy behavior was also examined. Risk-taking behaviors included using alcohol, smokeless tobacco, inhalants, marijuana, and other illicit drugs, binge drinking, smoking, drinking and driving, riding with a driver who had been drinking, sexual intercourse, shoplifting, vandalism, trouble with the police, hitting someone, hurting someone, using a weapon, group fighting, carrying a weapon for protection, threatening physical harm, truancy, gambling, eating disorders, depression, and suicide. This list of potential trouble for teens is gloomy. But adolescents who reported between 31 and 40 assets dealt with an average of only 1.1 of the negative behaviors listed above. Their peers who experience few developmental assets (zero to 10) struggled with an average of 9.5 of the risk-taking behaviors. Imagine a teen dealing with any nine of the negative behaviors listed above and a picture of a troubled teen emerges (Vermont Agency of Human Services, 1998).

Helping young adolescents construct assets

If communities are serious about providing their youth with the developmental assets, all segments of the public and private sector must lend their support. Individual citizens, civic organizations, houses of worship, and educational institutions all play important roles in providing youngsters with the advantages they need to flourish. Many communities have organizations such as Boys' and Girls' Clubs that provide positive support for youth. Coordinating efforts and resources around one common concept, such as that of developmental assets, provides focus for support, reducing the likelihood of duplicating efforts or leaving gaps in services rendered. For communities committed to providing developmental assets for their teen citizens, Benson, Galbraith, and Espeland (1997) envisioned the following conditions would be present:

- Parents will have access to training to strengthen their parenting skills and ability to provide assets.
- Youth organizations will do all they can to make their programs accessible to all young people.
- Communities will reach consensus on what values and norms should be passed down to youth.
- Teens will be encouraged to be actively involved and take on leadership roles in the community.
- Young people will interact with people from all age groups.
- All adults who work professionally with teens will receive professional training in asset building.
- Educators will attend to the affective needs of students as well as to their academic development.
- All community organizations and institutions will cooperate with each other for the benefit of kids. (p. 148)

While good programs that bolster young adolescents may require financial support, quality relationships with caring adults is the essential ingredient. Youth programs and institutions serve mainly as conduits to bring youngsters and nurturing adults together. It is the quality of the interpersonal relationships forged through association that makes the difference. "Asset-building is more about people than about programs." (Benson, Galbraith, & Espeland, 1997, p. 150). Others concur that high-quality relationships between teens and their adult associates is essential to help young adolescents mature in a positive manner. According to Scales (1996), young teens, especially those coming from disadvantaged backgrounds, are more likely to successfully navigate adolescence if they are surrounded by adults who

High-quality relationships between teens and their adult associates is essential to help young adolescents mature in a positive manner.

- See the genuine potential in youth.
- Put youth at the center of their programs.
- Believe they can make a difference with youth.
- See their contribution as something they owe the community.
- Are "unyieldingly authentic." (p. 41)

CASE STUDY

HOW SHOULD YOUNG ADOLESCENTS BE INVOLVED?

Students in Mr. Spencer's teacher advisory group frequently complained about having nothing to do after school. After hearing conversations about students loitering at the local mall and hanging out at friends' unsupervised homes, Mr. Spencer asked his advisees if they would like to organize a community service club. It would be up to the students to decide how to organize the club and what projects to sponsor. As the advisees realized that the proposed club would be their responsibility, their enthusiasm swelled. They first decided to volunteer their time to a nearby elementary school's after-school program. The students wrote a formal proposal to the school principal, outlining how their skills and interests would benefit the program. Each student committed to work three afternoons per week for an hour and a half each day tutoring younger students, supervising board games, assisting with handicraft sessions, and officiating intramural sports. At the end of the year, the elementary school principal honored the Community Service Club members for their help and contribution to making the after-school program successful.

Question:

Of the 22 Developmental Assets that middle schools can directly affect, which assets were addressed by the Community Service Club sponsored by Mr. Spencer's Advisory Group?

Comment:

Many Developmental Assets may be cultivated directly or indirectly by this after- school program. Specifically involved are the categories of empowerment, constructive use of time, values, and social competencies. As an advocate for young adolescents, Mr. Spencer recognized the need for his students to have a productive outlet for their talents and skills while providing them the autonomy to decide how to use their abilities.

Young adolescents deserve supportive communities and caring adult role models to guide them through the turbulent times of adolescence. They need adults to provide examples of what adult success looks like and give them the latitude and support to explore their own predilections. The purpose of asset development is more than a strategy to keep kids out of trouble, it is a way to promote positive outcomes and produce adolescents who will enter adulthood with a strong foundation that will enrich their lives and make them productive citizens.

In summary

Educators dedicated to teaching young adolescents have always sought to serve the whole child. While developing the intellect of young adolescents is the primary mission of middle schools, astute educators have long recognized academic achievement is impeded by lives that are in affective turmoil. By encouraging students to develop the internal assets available to them and facilitating access to external assets the community can provide, middle level educators can help young adolescents make good decisions and healthy choices. By attending schools where the educators promote resiliency and asset development, 10- to 15-year-olds can enjoy a happy and dynamic adolescence while setting the stage for a productive and rewarding adulthood.

While middle schools cannot complete the task of asset development in isolation, they have a key role to play that cannot adequately be fulfilled by others. By cooperating and collaborating with parents, religious institutions, and community organizations, middle schools can take the lead in helping to ensure that young adolescents have the assets they need to realize their full potential. ■

References

Adamczyk-Robinette, S., Fletcher, A., & Wright, K. (2002). Understanding the authoritative parenting–early adolescent tobacco use link: The mediating role of peer tobacco use. *Journal of Youth and Adolescence, 31*(4), 311–318.

Alexander, W. (2006). *Student-oriented curriculum: A remarkable journey of discovery.* Westerville, OH: National Middle School Association.

Allen, R. (2003). The democratic aims of service learning. *Educational Leadership, 60*(6), 51–54.

Anderson, C., & Bushman, B. (2002). Human aggression. *Annual Review of Psychology, 53,* 27–51.

Arnett, J. (1995). Adolescents' uses of media for self-socialization. *Journal of Youth and Adolescence, 24*(5), 519–533.

Arnett, J. (2004). *Adolescence and emerging adulthood: A cultural approach.* Upper Saddle River, NJ: Pearson Prentice Hall.

Arnold, M., Mackey, K., & Pratt, M. (2001). Adolescents' stories of decision making in more or less authoritative families: Respecting the voices of parents in narrative. *Journal of Adolescent Research, 16*(3), 243–268.

Aunola, K., Stattin, H., & Nurmi, J. (2000). Parenting styles and adolescent achievement strategies. *Journal of Adolescence, 23*(2), 205–222.

Baldwin, M., Keating, J., & Bachman, K. (2006). *Teaching in secondary schools today: Meeting the challenges of today's adolescents.* Upper Saddle River, NJ: Pearson Education, Inc.

Baldwin, S., & Hoffman, J. (2002). The dynamics of self-esteem: A growth-curve analysis. *Journal of Youth and Adolescence, 31*(2), 101–113.

Bandura, A. (2000). Self-efficacy. In A. Kazdin (Ed.), *Encyclopedia of psychology.* Washington, DC: American Psychological Association and New York: Oxford University Press.

Bardick, A., Dernes, K., McCulloch, A., Witko, K., Spriddle, J., & Roest, A. (2004). Eating disorder intervention, prevention, and treatment: Recommendations for school counselors. *Professional School Counseling, 8*(2), 168.

Baumrind, D. (1991). The influence of parenting style on adolescent competence and substance use. *Journal of Early Adolescence, 11*(1), 56–95.

Beane, J. (1993). *A middle school curriculum: From rhetoric to reality* (2nd ed.). Columbus, OH: National Middle School Association.

Beane, J. (2002) Beyond self-interest: A democratic core curriculum. *Educational Leadership. 59*(7), 25–28.

Beane, J. (2005). *A reason to teach: Creating classrooms of dignity and hope.* Portsmouth, NH: Heinemann.

Beane, J., & Lipka, D. (1987). *When the kids come first: Enhancing self-esteem.* Columbus, OH: National Middle School Association.

Becker, K., & Schmidt, M. (2005). When kids seek help on-line: Internet chat rooms and suicide. *The Journal of Strength-Based Interventions, 13*(4), 229.

Benson, P. (1997). *All kids are our kids: What communities must do to raise caring and responsible children and adolescents.* Minneapolis, MN: Search Institute.

Benson, P., Galbraith, J., & Espeland, P. (1997). *What kids need to succeed: Proven, practical ways to raise good kids.* Minneapolis, MN: Free Spirit Publishing, Inc.

Berger, K. (2006). *The developing person: Through childhood and adolescence.* New York: Worth Publishers.

Billig, S. (2000). Research on K–12 school-based service learning. *Phi Delta Kappan, 81*(9), 658–664.

Blyth, D., & Simmons, R. (1987). *Moving into adolescence.* Hawthorne, NY: Aldine de Gruyter.

Bradley, J. (1998, April 15). Muddle in the middle. *Education Week, 17*(31), 38–42.

Brodkin, A., & Coleman, M. (1996, May/June). What makes a child resilient? How you can help kids succeed against the odds. *Instructor, 105*(8), 28–29.

Brooks-Gunn, J., & Paikoff, R. (1993). Sex is a gamble, kissing is a game: Adolescent sexuality and health promotion. In S. Millstein, A. Petersen, & E. Nightingale (Eds.), *Promoting the health of adolescents: New directions for the twenty-first century* (pp. 180–208). New York: Oxford University Press.

Brown, A., & Flanigan, C. (Eds.). (2003). *Fourteen and younger: The sexual behavior of young adolescents* (Summary). Washington, DC: National Campaign to Prevent Teen Pregnancy.

Brown, J., & Schulze, L. (1990). The effects of race, gender, and fandom on audience interpretations of Madonna's music videos. *Journal of Communication, 40*, 88–102.

Brown, L., & Gilligan, C. (1990, April). *The psychology of women and the development of girls.* Paper presented at the Laurel-Harvard Conference on Psychology of Women and the Education of Girls, Cleveland, OH.

Buddy, J. (2005). Addressing the student health epidemic. *School Library Media Activities Monthly, 22*(2), 56–58.

Buhrmester, D. (2001, April). *Does age at which romantic involvement starts matter?* Paper presented at the meeting of the Society for Research in Child Development, Minneapolis, MN.

Bunte, A. (1996, March). Peers and peer pressure. *Message From the Middle: Newsletter from the Wisconsin Association for Middle Level Educators.*

Bushman, B., & Cantor, J. (2003). Media ratings for violence and sex: Implications for policymakers and parents. *American Psychologist, 58*(2), 130–141.

Caissy, G. (1994). *Early adolescence: Understanding the 10 to 15 year old.* New York: Insight Books/Plenum Press.

Carnegie Council on Adolescent Development. (1989). *Turning points: Preparing American youth for the 21st century.* New York: Carnegie Corporation.

Carnegie Council on Adolescent Development. (1996). *Great transitions: Preparing adolescents for a new century* (Abridged version). New York: Carnegie Corporation.

Carskadon, M. (1999). When worlds collide: Adolescent need for sleep versus societal demands. *Phi Delta Kappan, 80*(5), 348–353.

Carskadon, M. (2002). *Adolescent sleep patterns: Biological, social, and psychological influences.* Port Chester, NY: Cambridge University Press.

Centers for Chronic Disease Prevention. (2002). *Promoting lifelong healthy eating: An overview of Centers for Chronic Disease Prevention's Guidelines for school health programs.* (ERIC Document Reproduction Service No. ED 460 103).

Centers for Disease Control. (2002, September 27). Trends in sexual risk behaviors among high school students—United States, 1991–2001. *Morbidity & Mortality Weekly Report, 51*(38), 856–859. Retrieved June 3, 2007, from http://www.cdc.gov/mmwr/preview/mmwrhtml/mm5138a2.htm

Clasen, D., & Brown, B. (1990). Untitled brochure. Platteville, WI: Center for the Education of the Young Adolescent.

Cobb, C., & Mayer, J. (2000). Emotional intelligence: What the research says. *Educational Leadership, 58*(3), 14–18.

Cole, M. (1997). *Cultural psychology.* Cambridge, MA: Harvard University Press.

Conklin, M., Marshak, J., & Meyer, M. (2004). The role of the school nutrition environment for promoting the health of young adolescents. *Middle School Journal, 35*(5), 27–32.

Cookson, P. (2001). Fostering moral democracy. *Educational Leadership, 59*(2), 42–45.

Cotton, E. (2000). *The online classroom: Teaching with the internet* (4th ed.) Bloomington, IN: ERIC-REC/EdInfo Press.

Dacey, J., & Kenny, M. (1997). *Adolescent development.* Dubuque, IA: Brown and Benchmark.

Dale, D., & Van Staveren, T. (2004). Childhood obesity problems and solutions: Food choices and physical activity, at school and at home underlie the childhood obesity problem. What role can schools play in finding a solution? *Journal of Physical Education, Recreation, and Dance, 75*(7), 44.

Deitte, D. (2002). Character education provides focus for advisory. *Middle School Journal, 35*(1), 21–27.

Diamond, L., & Lucas, S. (2004). Sexual-minority and heterosexual youths' peer relationships: Experiences, expectations, and implications for well-being. *Journal of Research on Adolescence,14*(3), 313–340.

Dietz, T. (1998). An examination of violence and gender role portrayals in video games: Implications for gender socialization and aggressive behavior. *Sex Roles, 38,* 425–442.

Ebata, A. (1994). Helping young adolescents cope with stress. *School-age Connections, 4*(2), 1–3.

Eccles, J., & Midgley, C. (1989). Stage/environment fit: Developmentally appropriate classrooms for young adolescents. In R.E. Ames & C. Ames (Eds.), *Research on motivation and education* (Vol. 3, pp. 139–186). New York: Academic.

Egan, S., & Perry, D. (1998). Does low self-regard invite victimization? *Developmental Psychology, 34*(2), 299–309.

Elkind, D. (1976). *Child development and education: A Piagetian perspective.* New York: Oxford University Press.

Elkind, D. (1991). *The hurried child.* Reading, MA: Addison-Wesley.

Encyclopedia of Children's Health. (2007). *Sexually transmitted diseases.* Retrieved June 7, 2007, from http://health.enotes.com/childrens-health-encyclopedia/sexually-transmitted-diseases/print

Engeland, A., Bjorge, T., Tverdal, A., & Sogaard, A. (2004). Obesity in adolescence and adulthood and the risks of adult mortality. *Epidemiology, 15,* 79–85.

Erikson, E. (1968). *Identity: Youth and crisis.* New York: W.W. Norton.

Evans, E., Hawton, K., & Rodham, K. (2005). Suicidal phenomena and abuse in adolescents: A review of epidemiological studies. *Child abuse and neglect, 29*(1), 45–58.

Ference, R., & McDowell, J (2005). Essential elements of specialized middle level teacher preparation programs. *Middle School Journal, 36*(3), 4–10.

Findley, N. (2005). What do we mean by limited attention span? *Phi Delta Kappan, 86*(9), 652–653.

Finkelhor, D., Mitchell, K., & Wolak, J. (2000). *Online victimization: A report on the nation's youth.* Durham, NH: Crimes Against Children Research Center. Retrieved June 7, 2007, from http://www.unh.edu/ccrc/VictimizationOnlineSurvey.pdf

FLETEL Business Services. 2005. Retrieved June 13, 2007, from http://www.fletel.co.uk/doctors.html

Focus Adolescent Services. (2000). *Inhalant abuse: It's deadly.* Retrieved June 7, 2007, from http://www.focusas.com/Inhalants.html

Fox, K., Page, A., Peters, D., Armstrong, N., & Kirby, B. (1994). Dietary restraint and self-esteem in early adolescents. *Personality and Individual Differences, 17,* 87–96.

Franklin, J. (2005a). Mental mileage: How teachers are putting brain research to use. *Educational Update, 47*(6), 1–3, 7.

Franklin, J. (2005b). Removing the emotional roadblocks in education. *Education Update, 47*(11), 2–4, 8.

Friesch, R. (1984). Body fat, puberty, and fertility. *Biological Review, 59,* 161–188.

Gallup, G., & Bezilla, R. (1992). *The religious life of young Americans.* Princeton, NJ: Gallup Institute.

Gaskill, P. (2002). Progress in the certification of middle level personnel. *Middle School Journal, 33*(5), 33–40.

Ge, X., Conger, R., & Elder, G. (2001). The relationship between puberty and psychological distress in adolescent boys. *Journal of Research on Adolescence, 11*, 49–70.

Giannetti, C., & Sagarese, M. (2001). *Cliques: Eight steps to help your child survive the jungle.* New York: Broadway Books.

Giedd, J., Vaituzis, A., Hamburger, S., Lange, N., Rajapakse, J., Kayssen, D., et al. (1996). Qualitative MRI of the temporal lobe, amygdala, and hippocampus in normal human development: Ages 4–18 years. *Journal of Comparative Neurology, 366*(2), 223–230.

Gilligan, C. (1982). *In a different voice: Psychological theory and women's development.* Cambridge, MA: Harvard University Press.

Gilmartin, B. (2004). Myopia: Pathways to therapy. *Optometry and Vision Science, 81*(1), 1–3.

Goleman, D. (1995). *Emotional intelligence: Why it can matter more than IQ.* New York: Bantam Books.

Goodlad, J. (1984). *A place called school.* New York: McGraw Hill.

Gottman, J., & Parker, J. (Eds.). (1987). *Conversations of friends.* New York: Cambridge University Press.

Graham, S., & Juvonen, J. (1998). Self-blame and peer victimization in middle school: An attributional analysis. *Developmental Psychology, 34*(3), 587–99.

Greenberg, B., Siemicki, M., & Dorfman, S. (1986). *Sex content in r-rated films viewed by adolescents.* Project Cast Report #3. East Lansing, MI: Michigan State University

Gross, E. (2004). Adolescents and Internet use: What we expect, what teens report. *Journal of Applied Developmental Psychology: An International Lifespan Journal, 25*(6): 633–649.

Hallman, R. (1967). Techniques for creative teaching. *Journal for Creative Behavior, 1*(3), 325–330.

Harter, S. (1989). *Self-perception profile for adolescents.* Denver, CO: University of Denver, Department of Psychology.

Harter, S. (1993). Causes and consequences of low self-esteem in children and adolescents. In R.F. Baumeister (Ed.), *Self-esteem: The puzzle of low self-regard* (pp. 87–116). New York: Plenum Press.

Harter, S. (1996). The perceived directionality of the link between approval and self-worth: The liabilities of a looking glass self-orientation among young adolescents. *Journal of Research on Adolescence, 6*(3), 285–308.

Harter, S. (1999). *The construction of self.* New York: Guilford.

Harter, S., Waters., P., & Whitesell, N. (1996, March). *False self-behavior and lack of voice among adolescent males and females.* Paper presented at the meeting of the Society for Research on Adolescence, Boston, MA.

Hartup, W. (1983). The peer system. In P.H. Mussen (Ed.), *Handbook of child psychology* (4th ed., Vol 4). New York: Wiley Press.

Hayes, C. , & Morgan, M. (2005). Evaluation of a psychoeducational program to help adolescents cope. *Journal of Youth and Adolescence, 34*(2), 111.

Herman-Giddens, M., Slora, E., & Wasserman, R. (1997). Secondary sexual characteristics and menses in young girls seen in office practice: A study from the Pediatric Research in Office Setting Network. *Pediatrics, 99*, 505–512.

Hicks, L. (1997). How do academic motivation and peer relationships mix in an adolescent's world? *Middle School Journal, 28*(4), 18–22.

Hoffman, M. (1980). Moral development in adolescents. In J. Adelson (Ed.), *Handbook of educational psychology* (pp. 295–343). New York: Wiley.

Hogan, C., & Murphy, D. (2000). *Toward an 'economic of prevention': Illustrations from Vermont's experience.* Waterbury, VT: Vermont Agency on Human Services.

Hollingshead, A. (1975). *Elmtown's youth and Elmtown revisited.* New York: Wiley.

Ishizuka, K. (2005). Teens are tech wizards? Not! New study debunks stereotype of teens as tech experts. *School Library Journal, 51*(4), 24.

Jackson, A., & Davis, G. (2000). *Turning points 2000: Educating adolescents in the 21st century.* New York: Carnegie Corporation.

Jenkins, H. (2005). Getting into the game. *Educational Leadership, 62*(7), 48–51.

John-Steiner, V., & Mahn, H. (2003). Sociocultural context for teaching and learning. In W. M. Reynolds & G. E. Miller (Eds.), *Handbook of psychology* (Vol. 7) (pp. 125–151). New York: Wiley.

Jones, J. (2004). Media madness: With TV and the Internet available 24/7, can libraries compete? *School Library Journal, 50*(8), 32.

Kaiser Family Foundation. (2002). *Key facts: Teens online.* Menlo Park, CA. Henry J. Kaiser Family Foundation.

Kandel, D. (1975). Stages in adolescent involvement in drug use. *Science, 190,* 912–914.

Kandel, D. (2002). *Stages and pathways of drug involvement: Examining the gateway hypothesis.* New York: Cambridge University Press.

Kantrowitz, B., & Springen, K. (2005, December 12). A teen health gap. *Newsweek,* pp. 62, 65.

Kaplowitz, P., Slora, R,. Wasserman, R., Pedlow, M., & Herman-Giddens, M. (2001). Earlier onset of puberty in girls: Relation to increased body mass index and race. *Pediatrics 108,* 347–353.

Kastner, L., & Wyatt, J. (2004). Instant messaging: Managing the medium. *ParentMap: Monthly newsmagazine and online resource for Seattle and Eastside parents.* Retrieved July 4, 2004, from www.parentmap.com

Keith, S., & Martin, M. (2005). Cyber-bullying: Creating a culture of respect in a cyber world. *Reclaiming Children and Youth: The Journal of Strength Based Interventions, 13*(4): 224.

Kelly, T., Lynch, K., Donovan, J., & Clark, D. (2001). Alcohol use disorders and risk factor interactions for adolescent suicidal ideation and attempts. *Suicide and Life-Threatening Behavior, 31*(2), 181–193.

Kennedy, J. (1990). Determinants of peer social status: Contributions of physical appearance, reputations, and behavior. *Journal of Youth and Adolescence, 19,* 233–244.

Kidd, S., & Meyer, C. (2002, Spring). Similarities of school shootings in rural and small town communities. *Journal of Rural Community Psychology, E5*(1). Retrieved June 11, 2007, from http://www.marshall.edu/jrcp/sp2002/SP2002Contents.htm

Kielsmeier, J. (2000). Time to serve, time to learn. *Phi Delta Kappan, 81*(9), 652–657.

Kirby, D. (2000). What does the research say about sexuality education? *Educational Leadership, 58*(2), 72-75.

Knowles, T., & Brown, D. (2000). *What every middle school teacher should know.* Portsmouth, NH, Heinemann, and Westerville, OH: National Middle School Association.

Kooijmans., T. (2004). *Effects of video games on aggressive thoughts and behaviors during development.* Retrieved June 11, 2007, from www.personalityresearch.org/papers/kooijmans.html

Kuntz, S. (2005). *The story of alpha: A multiage student-centered team—33 years and counting.* Westerville, OH: National Middle School Association.

Lafontana, K., & Cillessen, A. (2002). Children's perceptions of popular and unpopular peers: A multimethod assessment. *Developmental Psychology, 38*(5), 635–647.

Lenhart, A., Rainie, L., & Lewis, O. (2002). *Teenage life online: The rise of the instant message generation and the Internet's impact on friendships and family relations.* Washington, DC: Pew Internet and American Life Project.

Lickona, T. (1991). *Educating for character: How our schools can teach respect and responsibility.* New York: Bantam.

Lickona, T. (1999). Religion and character. *Phi Delta Kappan, 81*(1), 21–27.

Lipka, R., Lounsbury, J., Toepfer, C., Vars, G., Alessi, S., & Kridel, C. (1998). *The Eight-Year Study revisited: Lessons from the past for the present.* Columbus, OH: National Middle School Association.

Loosli, A., & Ruud, J. (1998). Meatless diets in female athletes: A red flag. *Physician and Sports-medicine, 26*(11), 45–48.

Lundeberg, M., Fox, P., & Puncochar, J. (1994). Highly confident but wrong: Gender differences and similarities in confident judgments. *Journal of Educational Psychology, 86*, 114–121.

Manlove, J., & Terry, E. (2000). *Trends in sexual activity and contraceptive use among teens.* Washington, DC: The National Campaign to Prevent Teen Pregnancy.

Mann, L., Harmoni, R., & Power, C. (1989). Adolescent decision making: The development of competence. *Journal of Adolescence, 12*, 265–278.

Manning, L., & Bucher. K. (2001). *Teaching in the middle school.* Upper Saddle River, NJ: Prentice-Hall.

Marcia, J. (1980). Identity development. In J. Adelson (Ed.), *Handbook of adolescent psychology* (pp. 561–565). New York: Wiley.

Matthews, H., Taylor, M., Percy-Smith, B., & Limb, M. (2000). The unacceptable 'flaneur': The shopping mall as teenage hangout. *Childhood: A Global Journal of Child Research, 7*(3), 279–294.

Mayer, J., Caruso, D., & Salovey, P. (1999). Emotional intelligence meets standards for traditional intelligence. *Intelligence, 27*, 267–298.

McCullen, C. (2001). The electronic thread: Online resources for battling bullies. *Middle Ground: The Magazine of Middle Level Education, 5*(2), 7–9.

McGee, R., & Williams, S. (2000). Does low self-esteem predict health: Compromising behaviors among adolescents. *Journal of Adolescence, 23*(5), 569–582.

Mertens, S., Flowers, N., & Mulhall, P. (2003). Should middle grades students be left alone after school? *Middle School Journal, 34*(5): 57–61.

Meshel, D. (2004). Intergenerational contact, attitudes, and stereotypes of adolescents and older people. *Educational Gerontology, 30*(6), 457–479.

Meyer, M., Marshak, J., & Conklin, M. (2004). The role of the school nutrition environment for promoting the health of young adolescents. *Middle School Journal, 35*(5), 27–32.

Miga, A. (2005, November 30). Cannibalism in video game is denounced. *The Burlington Free Press*, p. 3A.

Molnar, A. (2004, December/January). Cashing in on the classroom. *Educational Leadership, 61*(4), 79–84.

Molnar, A. (2005). Ivy-covered malls and creeping commercialism. *Educational Leadership, 62*(5), 74–79.

National Drug Intelligence Center. (2002). *Prescription drug abuse and youth: Information brief.* (ERIC Document Reproduction Service No. ED 473 813)

National Mental Health Association. (2006). Adolescent depression: Helping depressed teens. Alexandria, VA. Retrieved June 14, 2007, from http://www.mentalhealthamerica.net

National Middle School Association.(2003). *This we believe: Successful schools for young adolescents.* Westerville, OH: Author.

National Middle School Association. (1997). *Research Summary 10. Sports in the Middle Grades.* Westerville, OH: Author. Retrieved June 11, 2007, from http://www.nmsa.org/Research/ResearchSummaries/tabid/115/

Nelson, G. (2001). Choosing content that's worth knowing. *Educational Leadership, 59*(2), 12–16.

New England League of Middle Schools. (1997, December). Facts about bullying. *Midlines.*

Newman, B., & Muzzonigro, P. (1993). The effects of traditional family values on the coming out process of adolescents. *Adolescence, 28*, 213–226.

Olweus, D. (2003). A profile of bullying at school. *Educational Leadership, 60*(6), 13–17.

Page, R., & Page, T. (2003). *Fostering emotional well-being in the classroom.* Sudbury, MA: Jones and Bartlett.

159

Pennington, A. (2004). *The hottest teen business for 2005*. Retrieved June 14, 2007, from http://www.entrepreneur.com/startingabusiness/businessideas/article73794.html

Petersen, A., & Stemmler, M. (2005). Gender differential influences of early adolescent risk factors for the development of depressive affect. *Journal of Youth and Adolescence, 34*(3), 175.

Piaget, J. (1954). *The construction of reality in the child*. New York: Basic Books.

Pope, D., & Simon, R. (2005). Help for stressed students. *Educational Leadership, 62*(7), 33–37.

Powell, S. (2005). *Introduction to middle school*. Upper Saddle River, NJ: Pearson Education, Inc.

Preboth, M. (2000). Marijuana use among children and adolescents. *American Family Physician, 63*(9), 2887.

Prensky, M. (2006). Listen to the natives. *Educational Leadership, 63*(4), 8–13.

Purkey, W., & Novak, J. (1996). *Inviting school success: A self-concept approach to teaching, learning, and democratic practice*. Belmont, CA: Wadsworth.

Renard, L. (2005). Teaching the DIG generation. *Educational Leadership, 62*(7), 44–47.

Rice, F. (1996). *The adolescent: Development, relationships, and culture*. Needham Heights, MA: Allyn and Bacon.

Roberts, D., & Foehr, U. (2004). *Kids and media in America: Patterns of use at the millennium*. New York: Cambridge University Press.

Roberts, D., Foehr, U., & Rideout, V. (2005). *Generation M: Media in the lives of 8–18 year-olds*. New York: Henry J. Kaiser Family Foundation.

Roberts, D., Foehr, U., Rideout, V., & Brodie, M. (2005). *Kids and the media at the new millennium: A comprehensive national analysis of children's media use*. New York: Henry J. Kaiser Family Foundation.

Santrock, J. (2003). *Adolescence* (9th ed.). New York: McGraw Hill.

Santrock, J. (2005). *Adolescence* (10th ed.). New York: McGraw Hill.

Satcher, D. (2005). Healthy and ready to learn. *Educational Leadership, 63*(1), 26–30.

Scales, P. (1996). *Boxed in and bored: How middle schools continue to fail young adolescents—and what good middle schools do right*. Minneapolis, MN: Search Institute.

Scales, P. (1999). Care and challenge: The sources of student success. *Middle Ground, 3*(2), 21–23.

Schaffer, D., Squire, K., Halverson, R., & Gee, J. (2005). Video games and the future of learning. *Phi Delta Kappan, 87*(2), 105–111.

Schlozman, S. (2001). Too sad to learn. *Educational Leadership, 59*(1), 80–81.

Schwimmer, J., Burkwinkle, T., & Varni, J. (2003). Health-related quality of life of severely obese children and adolescents. *Journal of the American Medical Association, 289*, 1813–1819.

Search Institute. (1997). *The asset approach: Giving kids what they need to succeed*. Minneapolis, MN: Author.

Simmons, R., Rosenberg, F., & Rosenberg, M. (1973). Disturbance in the self-image at adolescence. *American Sociological Review, 38*(5), 553–568.

Smetana, J., Yau, J., Restrepo, A., & Braeges, J. (1991). Conflict and adaptation in adolescence: Adolescent–parent conflict. In M. E. Colton & S. Gore (Eds.), *Adolescent stress: Causes and consequences* (pp. 43–65). New York: Aldine De Gruyter.

Society for Neuroscience. (2002). *Young brains on alchol: Brain briefings*. Retrieved June 14, 2007, from http://www.sfn. org/index/cfm?pagename=brainBriefings_youngBrainsOnAlcohol

Speck, P. (1995, Fall). My name by any other name is not myself. *Middle Ground, 6*–7.

Springer, M. (1994). *Watershed: A successful voyage into integrated learning*. Columbus, OH: National Middle School Association.

Springer, M. (2006). *Soundings: A democratic, student-centered education*. Westerville, OH: National Middle School Association.

State of Vermont. (2005). *School data and reports: Per pupil spending by school type, FY 2005 Report.* Retrieved June 13, 2007, from http://education.vermont.gov/new/html/maindata.html

Steinberg, A., & Wheelock, A. (1993). After tracking what? Middle schools find new answers. In A. Steinberg (Ed.), *Adolescents and schools: Improving the fit* (pp. 13-29). Cambridge, MA: Harvard Education Letter.

Steinberg, L. (1994). *Crossing paths: How your child's adolescence triggers your own crisis.* New York: Simon and Schuster.

Steinberg, L. (2001). We know some things: Parent-adolescent relationships in retrospect and prospect. *Journal of Research on Adolescence, 11*(1), 1–9.

Stevenson, C. (1998). *Teaching ten to fourteen year olds.* New York: Addison Wesley Longman.

Strasburger, V., & Wilson, B. (2002). *Children, adolescents, and the media.* Newbury Park, CA: Sage.

Stupak, N. (2004). *Positive effects of video games on development.* Retrieved June 11, 2007, from www.personalityresearch.org/papers/kooijmans.html

Swaim, J., & McEwin, C.K. (1997). Middle level competitive sports programs. In J. Irvin (Ed.), *What current research says to the middle level practitioner* (pp. 151–159). Columbus, OH: National Middle School Association.

Tyre, P. (2005, December 5). Fighting anorexia: No one to blame. *Newsweek,* pp. 51–59.

United States Department of Agriculture (1994–1996). *Continuing survey of food intakes for individuals* (CSFII). Washington, DC: Author.

United States Department of Health and Human Services. (2003). *Alcohol use by persons under the legal drinking age of 21.* Retrieved June 11, 2007, from http://oas.samhsa.gov/2k3/UnderageDrinking/UnderageDrinking.htm

United States Department of Education. (1998). *Annual report on school safety.* Retrieved June 13, 2007, from http://www.ed.gov/pubs/AnnSchoolRept98/index.html

United States Department of Justice, Bureau of Justice Statistics. (2002, April). *Prison and jail inmates at mid-year 2001.* Washington, DC: Author.

United States National Library of Medicine. (2005). *Death among children and adolescents.* Retrieved June 14, 2007, from http://www.aacap.org/cs/root/resources _for_families/child_and_adolescent_mental_illness_statistics

University of California, San Francisco. (2005). *Teens believe oral sex is safer, more acceptable to peers.* Retrieved June 11, 2007, from http://www.sciencedaily.com/releases/2005/04/050411135016.htm

University of Maine. (2005). *Sports done right. A call to action on behalf of Maine's student athletes.* Orono, ME: Author.

Van Hoose, J., Strahan, D., & L'Esperance, M. (2001). *Promoting harmony: Young adolescent development and school practices.* Westerville, OH: National Middle School Association.

Vars, G. (2001). Can curricular integration survive in an era of high-stakes testing? *Middle School Journal, 33*(2), 7–17.

Vermont Agency of Human Services. (1998). *Developmental assets: A profile of your youth.* Report Number 8172. Prepared by Search Institute, Minneapolis, MN.

Vermont Department of Education. (2000). *Vermont framework of standards and learning opportunities.* Montpelier, VT: Author.

Vermont Department of Education. (2005). *School data and reports: Per pupil spending by school type, FY 2005 report.* Montpelier, VT: Author.

Vermont Department of Health. (2005). *The 2005 Vermont youth risk behavior survey.* Burlington, VT: Author.

Vincent, P. (1999). *Developing character in students.* Chapel Hill, NC: Character Development Publishing.

Wahlstrom, K. (1999). The prickly politics of school starting time. *Phi Delta Kappan, 80*(5), 345–347.

Walker, J. (2002). *Adolescent stress and depression.* University of Minnesota Extension Service. Retrieved June 11, 2007, from http://www.extension.umn.edu/distribution/youthdevelopment/DA3083.html

Walsh, D. (2001). Video game violence and public policy. Retrieved June 11, 2007, from http://culturalpolicy.uchicago.edu/conf2001/papers/walsh.html

Walsh, D., (2004, November). *Brains, hormones, and behavior.* Paper presented at the annual conference of National Middle School Association, Minneapolis, MN.

Weilbacher, G. (2001). Is curriculum integration an endangered species? *Middle School Journal, 33*(2), 18–27.

Weissbourd, R. (2003). Moral teachers, moral students. *Educational Leadership, 60*(6), 6–11.

Werner-Wilson, R., Fitzharris, J., & Morrissey, K. (2004). Adolescent and parent perceptions of media influences on adolescent sexuality. *Adolescence, 39*(154), 303.

White, A. (2004). Alcohol and the adolescent brain. Retrieved June 11, 2007, from http://www.duke.edu/~amwhite/Adolescence/adolescent5.html

Wilson, L., & Horch, H. (2002). Implications of brain research for teaching young adolescents. *Middle School Journal, 34*(1), 57–61.

Wing, M. (2001). Including emotional intelligence in lessons: Blending heads, hearts, and spirits. *The Journal of the New England League of Middle Schools, 14*(1), 40–43.

Wolfe, P. (2001). *Brain matters: Translating research into classroom practice.* Alexandria, VA: Association for Supervision and Curriculum Development.

Wolfe, P. (2005). Advice for the sleep-deprived. *Educational Leadership, 62*(7), 39–40.

Wolin, S., & Wolin, S. (1993). *The resilient self.* New York: Villiard Books.

Wormeli, R. (2001). *Meet me in the middle: Becoming an accomplished middle level teacher.* Portland, ME: Stenhouse.

Wormeli, R. (2002). One teacher to another: Beating a path to the brain. *Middle Ground, 5*(5), 23-25.

Wormeli, R. (2003). *Day one and beyond: Practical matters for new middle level teachers.* Portland, ME: Stenhouse.

Young, E., & Fors, S. (2001). Factors related to the eating habits of students in grades 9–12. *Journal of School Health, 71*(10), 483–488.

Zirkel, P. (2003). Bullying: A matter of law? *Phi Delta Kappan, 85*(1), 90–91.

About National Middle School Association

Since 1973, National Middle School Association (NMSA) has been the voice for those committed to the education and well-being of young adolescents and is the only national association dedicated exclusively to middle level youth.

NMSA's members are principals, teachers, central office personnel, professors, college students, parents, community leaders, and educational consultants in the United States, Canada, and 46 other countries. A major advocacy effort is Month of the Young Adolescent. This October celebration engages a wide range of organizations to help schools, families, and communities celebrate and honor young adolescents for their contributions to society.

NMSA offers publications, professional development services, and events for middle grades educators seeking to improve the education and overall development of 10- to 15-year-olds. In addition to the highly acclaimed *Middle School Journal*, *Middle Ground* magazine, and *Research in Middle Level Education Online*, we publish more than 100 books on every facet of middle grades education. Our landmark position paper, *This We Believe*, is recognized as the premier statement outlining the vision of middle grades education.

Membership is open to anyone committed to the education of young adolescents. Visit www.nmsa.org or call 1-800-528-NMSA for more information.

CPSIA information can be obtained
at www.ICGtesting.com
Printed in the USA
FSHW011856030222
88092FS

9 781560 902119